Training Japanese Managers

Allen Dickerman
foreword by
Patrick M. Boarman

Published in cooperation with the
Center for International Business,
Pepperdine University,
Los Angeles and Malibu, California
Dr. Patrick M. Boarman, Director of Research

The Praeger Special Studies program—utilizing the most modern and efficient book production techniques and a selective worldwide distribution network—makes available to the academic, government, and business communities significant, timely research in U.S. and international economic, social, and political development.

Training Japanese Managers

PRAEGER SPECIAL STUDIES IN INTERNATIONAL ECONOMICS AND DEVELOPMENT

Praeger Publishers   New York   Washington   London

Library of Congress Cataloging in Publication Data

Dickerman, Allen Briggs, 1914-
   Training Japanese managers.

   (Praeger special studies in international economics and development)
   Published in cooperation with the Center of International Business, Pepperdine University, Los Angeles and Malibu, California, Dr. Patrick M. Boarman, Director of Research.
   Bibliography: p.
   1. Industrial management—Japan. 2. Executives, Training of—Japan. I. Title.
HD70.J3D5   658.4'00952   73-19443
ISBN 0-275-28828-5

PRAEGER PUBLISHERS
111 Fourth Avenue, New York, N.Y. 10003, U.S.A.
5, Cromwell Place, London SW7 2JL, England

Published in the United States of America in 1974
by Praeger Publishers, Inc.

All rights reserved

© 1974 by Praeger Publishers, Inc.

Printed in the United States of America

FOREWORD
Patrick M. Boarman

This book by Professor Allen B. Dickerman, who is Director of the International Management Development Department and Associate Professor of Management at Syracuse University, examines closely, yet tersely one important facet of the Japanese economic success story, namely, the Japanese art of management.

The evolution of Japanese management is traced from its beginnings in the Meiji Restoration (1868-1911) to the present. Attention is focused on the development of those special attitudes and practices of Japanese managers which were primarily responsible both for the steady growth of the Japanese economy prior to World War II and for its spectacular performance since then. The author distinguishes between those elements of Japanese management methods which are peculiar to Japanese culture and society and those which have been borrowed from Europe and the United States. A further distinction is drawn between those Japanese management techniques which might be profitably adopted by western countries in contrast with those which are probably not exportable. Most importantly, the study stresses the changes currently taking place in Japanese management philosophy in the context of the new social and political challenges facing Japan, both at home and in the international arena.

The study has a pragmatic orientation throughout, with a special emphasis on American business activity in Japan. It includes detailed information about the structure of business education and management training programs in Japan, investment opportunities open to foreigners, and guidelines for western businessmen interested in joint ventures.

Some of the many topics covered are:
- the "ringisho" decision-making process, which is one of consensus rather than decree;
- the role of the "catching up with the great powers" syndrome as it operates in Japanese industry;
- the various modalities in the striking cooperation between Japanese business and the Japanese government;
- the role of the Japanese emphasis on competition and excellence as the criteria for survival in the management educacation system;

Patrick M. Boarman is Director of Research, Center for International Business, Pepperdine University, Los Angeles and Malibu, California.

- the unique ability of the Japanese to assimilate and to improve upon foreign technology;
- the all-pervasive importance of the group and of "team-spirit" as contrasted with the western emphasis on the individual;
- the Japanese stress on long-term growth rather than short-run profits as the dynamics of the Japanese business system;
- the overriding role of "personal" and "non-logical" factors in Japanese management, as contrasted with the impersonal and analytical focus of U.S. methods;
- the Japanese obsession with quality control (for example, its "zero defects" program);
- the special problems American corporate executives face in dealing with their Japanese counterparts;
- the impact on Japan's less developed neighbors of Japanese management philosophy and techniques;

and many others.

The Center for International Business of Pepperdine University (Los Angeles and Malibu, California) is pleased to be sponsor of Professor Dickerman's study. The Center is a private, nonprofit research organization, specializing in fundamental research on the frameworks—economic, monetary, political, and cultural—within which international trade and business are conducted. In discharging this function, we have occasion to review many manuscripts dealing with the above subjects. We have rarely had the privilege of receiving a study as informative, as timely, and as well-written as is Professor Dickerman's. His notable achievement is to have covered a complex subject in a brief, well-organized, and easy-to-read narrative. Though there is certainly no dearth of studies of Japanese business, we believe this short treatise will find wide readership among those executives, academicians, government officials, and the public generally who want to know more about the roots of the Japanese economic miracle, but who do not have the time to wade through a heavy tome on the subject.

Los Angeles
Summer, 1974

PREFACE

Interest in Japanese management development was stimulated by Japanese executives who have come to Syracuse University as participants in the programs of its International Management Development Department and by a brief visit to Japan in 1968. In 1970, with the help of a travel grant from the Center for International Business, Pepperdine University, in Los Angeles, a three-month research study of management development in the Far East and Southeast Asia was undertaken.

Of the countries visited, Japan had been the most successful in training managers and creating a climate for rapid economic and industrial development. Other Asian countries with equal access to technology had found it difficult to develop managerial techniques, practices, and philosophies of the type which would stimulate effective growth. Success for these nations will depend upon their ability to follow Japan's example of harmonizing (adapting—not adopting) western management within the framework of the cultural heritage of their people.

Many scholars and managers both in Japan and the United States have contributed ideas and facts for this study. Particularly helpful were the comments and insight of Professor Robert J. Ballon, of Sophia University in Tokyo; Dr. Charles L. Hughes, Director of Corporate Personnel for Texas Instruments in Dallas, Texas; and Dr. Gordon T. Bowles, Professor Emeritus of Anthropology at Syracuse University. This study would not have been possible without the assistance of Dr. Arthur L. Peterson, Professor and Chairman of the Department of Political Science of Ohio Wesleyan University and Dr. Patrick M. Boarman, Director of Research, Center for International Business, Pepperdine University, who were instrumental in furnishing financial support and in providing encouragement at each step of the research as it progressed from rough notes to the final copy.

Syracuse University has been most generous in releasing time to undertake this research activity. A special debt of gratitude is due Mrs. Sarah Dollard, Mrs. Susan Ingles, and Mrs. Beth Ruddock who typed the manuscript.

CONTENTS

	Page
FOREWORD Patrick M. Boarman	v
PREFACE	vii
LIST OF CHARTS	x
LIST OF ABBREVIATIONS	xi

Chapter

1	WHY JAPAN?	1
2	THE MANAGEMENT MOVEMENT	2
	Notes	9
3	MANAGEMENT PRACTICES	10
	Organizational Structure	10
	Decision-Making	13
	Employee Relations	18
	Foreign Technology	20
	Notes	22
4	MANAGEMENT DEVELOPMENT	23
	University Programs	27
	Other Management Development Programs	29
	In-Company Training	32
	International Management Training	35
	Notes	39
5	THE AMERICAN CORPORATION IN JAPAN	41
	Notes	56

Chapter		Page
6	IMPLICATIONS FOR THE LESS DEVELOPED COUNTRIES	58
	Characteristics of Development	58
	Transfer of Technology	61
	The Role of Small-Scale Industry	64
	The Role of Government	65
	Education	67
	Distribution and Transportation	70
	Growth of Private Industry	73
	The Automotive Industry in Developing Countries	75
	The Role of International Establishments	78
	Notes	80
7	JAPANESE MANAGEMENT IN THE 1970s	82
	Environmental Problems	82
	Management Concepts	83
	Labor	87
	Forecasting the Future	88
	International Aspects	91
	Notes	98
BIBLIOGRAPHY		100
ABOUT THE AUTHOR		105

LIST OF CHARTS

Chart		Page
Chart 1	Organizational Structure	12
Chart 2	Toyota Motor's Training System	33
Chart 3	Toyota Motor's Training Program	34
Chart 4	Toshiba's Training Program	36
Chart 5	Organization of the School System	68

LIST OF ABBREVIATIONS

APO	Asian Productivity Organization
CIOS	Conseil International pour L'organisation Scientifique
CSS	Civil Communications Section
GNP	Gross National Product
IBAM	Institute of Business Administration and Management
IESC	International Executive Service Corps
IMAJ	International Management Association of Japan
IMCC	International Management Cooperation Committee
JIBA	Japan Institute of Business Administration
JMA	Japan Management Association
MITI	Ministry of International Trade and Industry
MTM	Method Time Measurement
MTP	Management Training Program
MVE	Japanese Management Volunteer Executives
OECD	Organization for Economic Cooperation and Development
OTCA	Overseas Technical Cooperation Agency
SCAP	Supreme Commander of Allied Powers
TWI	Training Within Industry
UNCTAD	United Nations Conference on Trade and Development
WF	Work Factor
ZD	Zero Defects Program

Training Japanese Managers

CHAPTER 1

WHY JAPAN?

In the Far East, Japan not only has taken the lead in adapting western management to its economy, but also, since World War II, has achieved a growth rate which has moved its per capita income from 20th place to close to first place. Consequently, because of the significant influence of Japan on the economy of the Far East and more recently on the world, an analysis of Japanese management is important to an understanding of Japan and its relationship to industrial and economic development.

Four significant areas concerning management are particularly relevant to Japan. One is the management movement by means of which Japan has absorbed Western technology and management know-how. A second concerns the management practices of Japanese firms, particularly with regard to organizational structure, decision-making, and personnel administration. A third important factor is the selection and training of managers which will be described in the section devoted to management development. Since part of the focus of this study is on the development of foreign nationals for U.S. multinational corporations, a fourth topic is that of the effect of Japanese management traditions on the operating affiliates of U.S. corporations in Japan.

Because Japan has been successful in attaining a high degree of industrial and economic development, the means by which this has been accomplished should be of significance to the less developed nations which are seeking a better standard of living for their people. The rapid development of Japan resulted in many changes during the decade of the 1960s. In the 1970s, even more rapid changes are taking place in governmental policies and managerial thinking and practices: Japan's industrialization has created internal problems, and its sudden switch from a debtor to a creditor nation has caused revisions in its international economic policies.

CHAPTER 2

THE MANAGEMENT MOVEMENT

From 1639 until the signing of a Treaty of Friendship between the Tokugawa Bakufu government and Commodore Matthew Perry of the United States in 1854, Japan remained rather completely isolated from the rest of the world except through the Dutch factory on Dejima Island in the harbor of Nagasaki. Although during this isolationist period the Tokugawa Shogunate maintained a feudalistic structure and followed a policy of prohibiting all contacts with foreigners, the Dutch instructed the young scions of the feudal houses to understand the Dutch language, through which they gained access to the knowledge of the West and world events in Europe and later America. In Kyoto there was an academy run by some of the Japanese who had learned from the Dutch. Although the ability to read and write was quite widespread, only a few of the privileged classes enjoyed higher education. For example, at the Academy in Kyoto only about 100 of the elite future leaders were admitted at any one time. Some contact with the outside world was also maintained through a substantial Chinese colony in Nagasaki.

During this feudalistic period the economy remained relatively stable, not only through the maintenance of a fairly static population but also because the system was based upon rice quotas. Each feudal lord was permitted to produce so much rice and no more. Lords were ranked by title which equated so many sacks of rice to a given rank. (One might be known as a 20,000 rice lord.) Under this kind of system the feudal economy could not expand. The eventual collapse of the Tokugawa Shogunate in 1868 and the restoration of the Emperor Meiji resulted in the abolition of feudalism and the opening up of Japan to western culture.

The Meiji period (1868-1911) has been referred to by historians as a Restoration,[1] not a revolution of the masses from below, but a recognition by the leaders that a new course was needed for Japan, one which would mobilize resources for modernization, industrialization, and international trade. The mission of the new government was to replace the traditional feudal system with an adaptation of European civilization in such a way that Japan could become a modern, powerful, independent nation free from the threat of colonization by western powers.

Initially, it was anticipated that the large merchants of Tokyo, who controlled even the feudal lords through loans, would be the leaders in the new development. However, since these big merchants had become accustomed to their positions as heads of monopolistic organizations under relatively stable conditions of isolation, they were extremely conservative and feared any change. Consequently, even though the Meiji government encouraged them to take the leadership in developing a modern economy, they were reluctant to do so. As a result, the establishment of Japan's modern economy was left to enterprising groups who could understand the western economy and its advantages and profitability for Japan. The only class possessing higher education was the bushi (samurai) who traditionally looked down upon commerce and industry. As the rice economy stagnated and these samurai elite were reduced to poverty and heavy indebtedness, intermarriage with rich mercantile families became a way of relieving their destitution and led to a gradual change in attitude. They further justified their entrance into commerce and industry on the basis that it was not primarily for individual profit, but for the national interest and the retention of earnings to build a strong independent country.

From the standpoint of management development in Japan, three significant reforms were introduced during the Meiji Restoration. First was the change in political structure which permitted anyone regardless of family background to enter government service, business, or the military and to advance to a high position. Actually, the big family lords who remained loyal to the Emperor were given commoner titles such as baron, count, or marquis and in fact, the head of the Tokugawa family was made a prince. They received substantial stipends as peers of the new realm and formed the upper house in the new government. A second change was the introduction of the corporate form of organization and financing of the large enterprises through small capital investments by many. The former feudal lords also took advantage of the corporate form to invest part of their stipends in new industries and in commercial enterprises. As a third reform, education was made compulsory as a means of strengthening the national consciousness and an understanding of modern civilization. Universities and polytechnical schools were added resulting in a several fold increase in the number of university students between 1890 and 1940. Practically from the beginning of the Meiji period, students were free to enter any university or other institutions of higher learning. Since promotion in industry was based on education and ability, regardless of social position or place of birth, young people sought education. This, combined with a homogenous race maintained for more than 2,000 years, contributed to the rapid economic development and political stability of the country.*

As early as 1872 the Meiji government began employing foreign experts to take charge of Japan's industrialization and modernization. During the next thirty years the number of foreign experts coming to Japan to work for the government alone exceeded 6,000. These advisors from Europe and the United States were active not only in industry, but also in education, the military, medicine, finance, and diplomacy. As a result, by the end of the nineteenth century Japan had absorbed much of the leading western technology into its military and civilian cultures.[2]

In the beginning of the Meiji Restoration the government initiated industrialization by setting up model enterprises under state sponsorship. The private businessman was familiar with commercial activities but did not want to take the risk of producing industrial goods. In some instances, the government imported the whole production process including new materials, machinery, engineers, and technicians as well as sending Japanese to the Western Hemisphere to learn engineering and management.

From 1870 until World War II, Japanese management increasingly applied European and American technology in fabricating imported materials into exportable finished products. During this period in many phases of its development, Japan tended to imitate and adopt western technology. Commercial banking and cotton spinning were strongly influenced by English experts, as was the architecture of many of the buildings. The French and the Scotch built the first shipyards and a French engineer designed the first mechanized silk thread factory. Procelain manufacturing and the chemical industries were developed by German experts. The French influenced civil law and the Germans, public law and the constitution. Accounting systems came primarily from the Germans. After the publication of Taylor's Scientific Management, the influence of the American management methods became stronger in Japan, and much emphasis was placed on efficiency.

Western culture, as opposed to techniques, was introduced primarily in the public domain in such systems as government,

---

*For much of this background on social structure and political change, the author is indebted to Dr. Gordon T. Bowles, Professor Emeritus of Anthropology at Syracuse University.

education, justice, and, to a certain extent, in the economy which was divided between external industry and trade and internal subsistence. The agricultural areas were often self-contained and largely independent of urban industrialization except for the effects of the shift in manpower, improved transportation, and changes in governmental policies.

By the end of the Meiji era in 1911, light industry, of a crude rather than precision nature, was internationally competitive. Japan's basic chemical and heavy industries, on the other hand, were rather weak and unable to compete with those of the United States and Europe. With the advent of World War I, Europe's semimonopoly in producing and exporting industrial goods was destroyed and Japan was in an excellent position to take advantage of this market and to add to its industrial progress.

In 1920, Japan experienced an economic panic followed by an earthquake in the Kanto area in 1923 and a financial panic in 1927. Japan's economy suffered further because of the U.S. depression of 1929. This caused the Japanese Ministry of Commerce to establish the Industrial Rationalization Board in 1930. The Board's duties included the standardization of industrial products through the formation of cartels similar to those of Germany. In addition, the Board undertook the modernization of management by recommending the application of the scientific methods of the United States and the practices of American industry. The Board's Financial Committee standardized accounting practices along German principles and these were later widely adopted by Japanese enterprises. Most of the early professors of business administration in Japan were accountants who were influenced by German theories of management. However, in actual business management, Japanese companies employed American methods, not German.

In fact, within industry itself, American management methods began to replace British and German technology in Japan after the translation and publication of Taylor's Scientific Management in 1913. The spinning industry was the first to adopt some of Taylor's approach. Later applications were made in such areas as pharmaceuticals, cosmetics, footwear, machinery, and railway repair. A pioneer in stimulating the application of American scientific methods was Yoichi Uyeno who in 1921 became head of the Industrial Efficiency Institute of Japan. Uyeno went to the United States and Europe where he met with Frank and Lillian Gilbreth, F. W. Taylor, William Leffingwell (office management), and Harrington Emerson. Upon his return he expanded the functions of the Industrial Efficiency Institute to include lectures, publications, consultations, technical assistance, technical training in time and motion study, aptitude tests, and efficiency research. As a result of these expanded activities, the organization later became the Japan Federation of Efficiency Associations.

Another early leader of Japan's management movement was Nobuo Noda, Professor Emeritus of Seikei University, who in 1968 was awarded the Taylor Key by the Society for the Advancement of Management for his significant contributions to the management movement. Noda was primarily responsible for the drafting of the recommendation of the Production Management Committee of Japan's Industrial Rationalization Board. In order to disseminate its recommendations, the Japan Industries Association, a private organization, was formed. In 1942 this organization merged with Uyeno's Federation of Efficiency Associations to form the Japan Management Association (JMA), the largest management consulting firm in the country and a leading organization in top and middle management training.

However, in general, during the period from 1930 to the end of World War II, Japan made limited progress. The controlling power shifted from the financial and political groups to the military and the bureaucrats. Management knowledge was exchanged, but basic emphasis was on cost-reduction and efficiency and only a few progressive enterprises showed real interest in the management movement. Once the military was in complete control, all efforts were directed toward mass production of war goods.

Japan's defeat in World War II and consequent occupation by American forces had an influence on its industrial prosperity of today. Along with the defeat went Japan's policy of extending its power through military occupation and this was replaced with a concentration on economic development and penetration for the good of Japan.

In addition, the war had virtually destroyed the old industries of the country. This necessitated the building of new production facilities, permitting Japan to start over again industrially with the most modern technology and patents from abroad. The achievements of Japan during the first ten years after the war were outstanding and served as the base for the country's continued development both domestically and internationally.

The occupation by American forces immediately following the war also had an impact on Japan's industrial management. SCAP (Supreme Commander of Allied Powers) initiated efforts to establish a democratic industrial economy in Japan. In order to achieve greater uniformity in financial statements, SCAP formed a committee under the leadership of Professor Ohta to improve accounting practices and procedures.

SCAP also initiated a CCS (Civil Communications Section) training program for managers of Japanese communication equipment makers. American company practices were introduced dealing with policy formulation, organization principles, management systems, and operating problems. These lectures, although aimed at one industry, attracted wide attention and were published for nationwide distribution.

TWI (Training Within Industry) and MTP (Management Training Program) were also introduced by SCAP. The TWI series was popularized by Japan's Labor Ministry and was widely used in helping train Japanese workers.

As time went on, the larger companies and banks developed their own training institutes. Programs in these institutes are adaptations of American training methods. Case studies and group discussions were the two most widely used techniques in Japanese industrial training. The Hitachi Company and Toyota Motors both have outstanding, comprehensive, in-house training programs comparable in quality to those of any of the largest U.S. corporations.

Peter Drucker's <u>Practice of Management</u>, translated to Japanese in 1956, was widely read by Japanese businessmen and influenced their thinking on the objectives of management and the corporations. Quality control assumed strategic importance in Japanese industry after a 1950 lecture tour by Professor W. E. Deming. In fact, the leading business paper of Japan and the Union of Japanese Scientists and Engineers established an annual Deming Prize to be awarded to the company with outstanding achievement in statistical quality control.

Industrial engineering's contribution of Work Factor (WF) and Methods Time Measurement (MTM) are also popular in Japan and much research was done in establishing master standard times for welding, painting, forging, heat treating, and casting, in addition to the standard Work Factor values for elemental movements such as walking and lifting.

Additional stimulation of the management movement in Japan occurred in 1954, when four leading business organizations in Japan, <u>Keidanren</u>, the Federation of Economic Organizations; <u>Nikkeiren</u>, the Federation of Japanese Employers Organizations; the Japan Chamber of Commerce and Industry; and <u>Keizai Doyukai</u>, the Japan Committee for Economic Development agreed to establish the Japan Productivity Center in cooperation with the U.S. government's technical assistance program. Groups from all sectors of industry were sent to the United States to study management philosophy, productivity, marketing, and other aspects of management; and American specialists were brought to Japan. Programs of the Center included lectures, seminars, and committees, as well as the publication of magazines and reports, and presentation of radio and television programs, to mobilize Japanese industry's interest in productivity. The Center in Tokyo added a Productivity Research Institute in 1956, with a library of approximately 30,000 volumes. Since 1965, the Japan Productivity Center has operated an Academy of Management Development which conducts courses and seminars on all phases of business management and computer technology.

The Center has also worked cooperatively with unions and management with programs of courses, consultation, discussions, and committee activities. The Center encouraged the formation of the Japan Marketing Association, the Japan Materials Handling Society, the Japan Institute of Industrial Engineering, the Japan Consumer's Association, and the Japan Package Institute. The Japan Productivity Center is supported principally by income from the many seminars and courses it conducts, plus an annual membership fee from its 10,000 members, most of which are corporations. The Center has branches located throughout Japan and is the largest management training organization in the country.

In 1961, under the stimulation of the Japan Productivity Center, the Asian Productivity Organization (APO) was formed with headquarters in Tokyo. Initially, productivity centers in eight countries, Korea, Republic of China, Philippines, Thailand, India, Pakistan, Nepal, and Japan joined together in this cooperative effort to contribute to productivity and to raise the living standards of the people of Asia. Eventually, six other countries joined to make a total of fourteen member nations in the Asian Productivity Organization.

The most sophisticated and internationally recognized management association in Japan is the Japan CIOS Association, also know as the International Management Association of Japan. Its periodical, Management Japan, is published in English and with a worldwide circulation of 18,000 (4,000 in the United States) serves as a means of disseminating Japanese management concepts and philosophy to other parts of the world. In 1969, this organization hosted the 15th CIOS International Management Congress.

Most of the development of Japan was internal resulting in various improvements and innovations in industry within the country. In the 1960s, international expansion leading to overseas economic activities made it necessary for management to plan and develop the enterprise from a worldwide standpoint. Expansion of trade, overseas capital investment, and the liberalization of foreign investments within Japan itself broadened the scope of management with emphasis on internationalization of the enterprise.

Guiding this internationalization process has been the Ministry of International Trade and Industry (MITI), an influential force in modernizing Japan through the Management Committee of its Industrial Structure Deliberation Council which joined with the Production Management Committee of the Industrial Rationalization Board in 1964. This committee produced a number of documents relating to management. MITI also has encouraged seminars to improve marketing techniques, particularly in international trade.

Management in Japan has also focused its attention on the use of computers to build enterprises into a completely unified system.

Japan's corporations are already utilizing computers for planning and systematizing their various corporate divisions.

In summary, therefore, since the restoration of the Emperor Meiji in 1868, Japan has absorbed western management culture. The modernization was extraordinarily smooth from the social viewpoint because of the basic characteristics of the Japanese who accept whatever ways contribute to growth and development. Japan enjoys a deep sense of identity combined with a willingness to adapt to new conditions as necessary for survival. Industrialization and modernization have gone far beyond the level needed for survival to a position of approaching, for its people, the highest standard of living in the world.

NOTES

1. Robert J. Ballon, "Understanding the Japanese, Preparation for International Business," Business Horizons, volume 13 no. 3 (June 1970): p. 22.

2. See Nobuo Noda, How Japan Absorbed American Management Methods.

CHAPTER

3

MANAGEMENT PRACTICES

Japanese management is based upon value systems and employs practices that are somewhat different from those of American society with its emphasis on rationalization, money, individualism, mobility, and impersonalization. That such a system may work well in the United States does not mean that it is equally effective in Japan or other societies. Japan's institutions and managerial practices have certain peculiarities which are unique to Japanese culture and which have contributed to the country's development. Of particular significance are such aspects as organizational structure both among and within the firms, the decision-making process, and employee relations. All of these have had an effect on management development and on foreign investment and operations in Japan.

ORGANIZATIONAL STRUCTURE

With regard to national associations or organizations in Japan, the four most influential are the Federation of Economic Organizations (Keidanren), the Federation of Japanese Employers Organizations (Nikkeiren), the Japan Committee for Economic Development (Keizai Doyukai), and the Japan Chamber of Commerce and Industry. The Association for Medium and Small Enterprises is also an important management organization but does not have as strong a political influence as the other four.[1]

Keidanren is a federation of large enterprises organized for the purpose of studying economic policy and making suggestions to the government. Nikkeiren, on the other hand, is primarily concerned with labor policy and dealing with unions. Keizai Doyukai is made up of approximately 1,000 active individual businessmen representing the economy as a whole. Its basic objective is to encourage study and research on those activities related to the sound development of the economy and, in this respect, it fosters working relationships between the industrial world and academic circles. Keizai Doyukai, since 1961, has cooperated closely with the U. S. Committee for Economic Development and similar organizations in Europe and Australia. The Japanese Chamber of Commerce and Industry is a federation of the 139 member chambers in Japan and 46 abroad. Its functions include suggestions to government, investigating causes of economic problems, and serving as a sort of economic council to government.

In addition, the Kansai district of the Osaka-Kobe area has its own regional economic association (Kankeiren), the functions of which are similar to the nationwide Keidanren, and it does exercise some political influence in its area. The former private club-like organizations made up of businessmen and politicians such as the Japan Industry Club have been mostly absorbed by the Keizai Doyukai,

Prior to World War II, Japanese industry was dominated by the zaibatsu, which was officially broken up by the American occupation forces by putting new younger Japanese managers in the top executive positions of the major companies. In effect, however, the ties that bound the zaibatsu together were never really broken and they have become groups of companies under what is currently known as keiretsu. These groups consist of those companies organized around the former zaibatsu names such as Mitsubishi (28), Mitsui (22), Sumitomo (15), and those held together by the large banks such as Fuji, Dai-ichi and the Industrial Bank of Japan. The figures in parenthesis give some idea of the size of the groups but the actual number in each group may be a hundred or more when one takes into consideration the number of subcontractors and other small companies dependent upon the keiretsu parent for survival. For a foreign company expecting to do business in Japan, it is important to learn to which the group its prospective partner belongs and the latter's position within the group.[2]

The organizational structure of the Japanese company itself differs somewhat from the American style. (See Chart I for a summary illustration of a Japanese company's organizationsl structure.) Each company has a legally-required, ceremonial board of directors which, in effect, duplicates the management hierarchy of the company and to be a member is primarily a matter of social rank and favor rather than that of decision-making as such.

The top decision-making body is the company's managing directors and the president. The managing directors are operating heads of the various divisions and plants of the company. The rigid vertical structure of the Japanese company sometimes results in weak horizontal coordination and the managing board is designed to provide such coordination. The president, who may be the founder, son, or,

CHART 1

ORGANIZATIONAL STRUCTURE

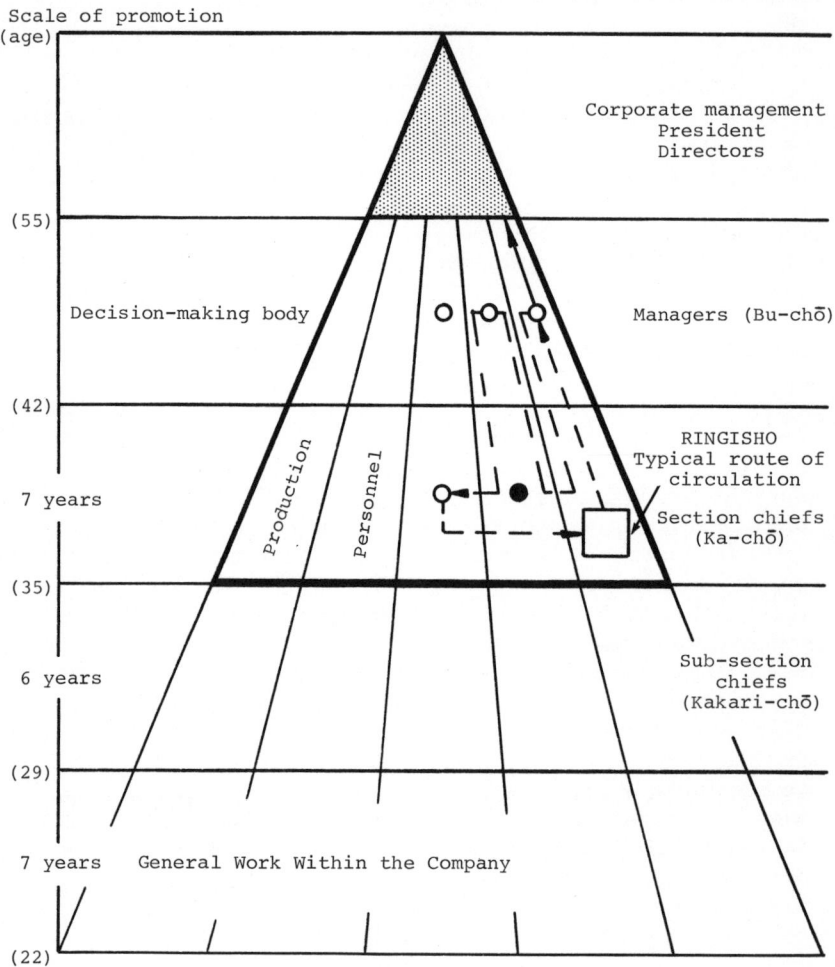

Source: Robert J. Ballon, Doing Business in Japan (Tokyo: Sophia University, 1967), p. 168.

son-in-law of the founder, or a person who has come up through the ranks of management is in most instances the chief executive officer. As such, he is expected to provide leadership for the company. Leadership from the standpoint of the Japanese consists of acceptance by the group and sharing in the "mutual emotional commitment within the group."3

Surrounding the president of a corporation is an intimate group of senior managers who look to him for leadership. These managers in turn provide leadership for groups reporting to them. The function of the president is primarily, therefore, to provide motivation through personnel rather than profits alone. It is his responsibility to select the best personnel and to insure their training and placement in positions where they can contribute to the development of the company. In this respect, the president is expected to be much more concerned with the human resources of the organization and their effective utilization than with the company's other resources which are generally the responsibility of various directors. The president also maintains contacts with the financial, governmental, and other institutions with which the company must deal in order to operate successfully. Another important function of the president is to select and prepare a successor for the presidential position and to hand the office of the presidency over to him at the appropriate time.

Titles such as director, division head, and section head are important in Japanese society and frequently have more prestige value than salary. In fact, a foreign businessman in Japan may have difficulties in getting the consideration he deserves if his title is translated as being unimportant.

Specialized staff functions tend to be weak in Japanese firms. The seniority system and the vertical organizational structure makes staff work a dead-end occupation. Many of the highly-trained, dynamic young people, rather than serving as advisors to top managers, are working in low-line positions because of their age and lack of seniority. Some large firms have organizational charts showing a line-and-staff organization, but it is questionable whether the actual operations do follow the charted organizational structure.

DECISION-MAKING

From the standpoint of policy-making, the Board of Directors is the final decision-making body but the actual power of the Board is concentrated in a few senior directors of the corporation who have hand-picked other directors from among the managing directors of the company. As previously indicated, much of the day-to-day management and decision-making is carried on by the managers of the various plants and even presidents of affiliated companies, many of whom may be represented on the Board. Final policy decisions, therefore, tend to reflect the thinking of the senior executive officer and a few of his close associates.

Another characteristic of Japanese management is the ringisho system, whereby decision-making is a continuous process of communication and participation throughout the entire organization. Almost every company in Japan employs this system in one form or another. Under this system, a plan or proposal is instituted by someone in the lower or middle management level. Before this plan is submitted to a higher official, it is reviewed by other departments at this same organizational level. In each department, and as it moves vertically through this organization, confirmation and authorization is indicated by having each responsible person affix his seal. In this way, ideas and plans are developed at middle management levels among men who are working at the same level. All are given an opportunity to make a contribution and by the time the final document reaches top management it represents the unanimous consent on the part of the individuals and departments affected in such a way that the recommendations are generally approved by top management. The system results in the delegation of part of the decision-making process to the level of management requiring coordination in putting plans into action.

The ringisho system is also illustrative of the difference between Japanese and western decision-making. In western culture, emphasis in decision-making is placed on a logical analysis of the factors involved in order to find an answer to a problem. In Japan, however, the most important aspect of the decision is defining the problem, which, in turn, determines whether a decision needs to be made. During the process, no consideration is given to possible solutions, in order to avoid forcing the people involved to take sides. By focusing on the problem rather than the answer, a consensus can be reached as to whether or not a problem exists which requires a change.[4]

Decision-making by consensus historically has had a special meaning in Japanese society. Idealistically, in a patriarchal situation, there should be much discussion so engineered by the leader that all are given a chance to have their "say." They should be called upon in proper age-seniority sequence with each rank or status represented in the meeting. When all have had their "says" and "counter says," the leader should then summarize the arguments for and against the probable results which might ensue in each case and then deftly produce a "solution" decision which would represent reasonable compromises, including actions to be taken by all sides to effect a total compromise, This kind of decision-making process allows considerable leeway for flexibility as well as for control.

Although such a decision-making process may require time, the actual implementation of the course of action is rapid. By the time all have agreed on the nature of the problem, the result is that no one in the organization needs to be convinced that a change is needed. The final course of action is determined by top management by referring the problem to the appropriate department for solution. In the process of defining the problem, it has already become evident as to where in the organization cooperation and resistance may occur, with the result that the answer does not have to be "sold" but merely adapted to the plans and operations of the departments concerned. In other words, the most important aspect of the Japanese decision-making process is deciding on the full range of alternatives without a commitment to any specific recommendation. In this way, the alternatives have been thoroughly discussed before action is taken, thereby making it easier for full agreement and cooperation in carrying out the decision. It is the noncommitment to alternatives that may result in a complete reversal of the decision at a later date with no "logical" (to the western mind) reason for the reversal.

As the Japanese are confronted by new situations, most important is the survival and growth of the enterprise and Japan itself. This management philosophy began with the entrepreneurs of the Meiji era who placed national interest ahead of self-interest. Modern development of Japan represents the result of the pride which management has taken in achieving the national goal of catching up with the advanced countries.

Relations between government and business in Japan have been directed toward encouraging economic and industrial development in such a way that it is frequently difficult to define the boundary between government and business in any given business decision. Japan's Economic Planning Agency works through a number of committees with representatives from business, industry and the academic community, as well as interested government agencies and committees in developing five and ten year plans which represent efforts to define in some detail the direction that the economy can most efficiently take. Policies reflecting these plans are developed and implemented primarily by the Ministry of International Trade and Industry and the Ministry of Finance through consulting committees made up of representatives of business and government. Through a wide range of formal and informal channels of communication between government and business, the policy decisions of these ministries tend to be more a matter of consensus than government decree.

This relationship between government and business has been described as "Japan, Incorporated,"[5] an expression which some Japanese resent as equivalent to "economic animal," which depicts Japan as an undesirable species with strong economic obsessions.

In comparison with the large multinational corporations of the United States and Western Europe, the Japanese feel that their companies operating overseas might better be described as "economic insects" feeding on what is left over. In fact, by the beginning of the 1970s the overseas investment of Japan was estimated as $4.5 billion as compared to $78 billion for the United States and a total of $128 billion for member countries of the Organization for Economic Cooperation and Development (OECD).[6] The government-industry relationship in Japan stems from socioeconomic characteristics that contribute to a strong national cohesion which yields a structure of government-business cooperation highly favorable for a systems approach to economic development.

A condition which helps create a unified approach to development is the similarity in training and education among the top men in government, industry, and financial institutions in Japan. Traditionally, government positions are considered socially desirable in Japan and, therefore, the government is able to attract outstanding graduates from the more prestigious universities. Industry and banks also recruit from these same institutions of higher learning with the result that the top officials in government, industry, and banks are graduates of a selected few universities, a condition described as gakubatsu (school cliques). Another condition which contributes to cooperation between government and industry is the retirement of government officials to directorships in business, the retirement of business executives to advisory positions in government, and the movement of top executives between banking institutions and industry.

Banks provide a much greater portion of the capital of Japanese companies than is common in western economies. As much as eighty percent or more of the capital requirements of many of the large corporations in Japan is supplied through bank loans. Rapid expansion can, therefore, take place through increased borrowing rather than reinvestment of earnings. Although many of the loans from the commercial bank may be considered short-term, they are frequently guaranteed by the Bank of Japan and are essentially long-term capital with the requirement that the company pay only the interest. Debt guarantees by the Bank of Japan do not apply to the smaller, less efficient companies thereby tending to encourage concentration of production in the larger, more efficient firms. Since large corporations are indirectly dependent upon the Bank of Japan through its loan guarantees, legal reserve requirements, open-market operations, and discount rates, the government can have an influence on the growth of any particular company. However, since growth is financed from loans rather than retained earnings, a company can expand rapidly at prices which yield a nominal profit margin sufficient to cover interest and a similar return on a small stockholder equity.

Although the policies and practices of Japan's financial institutions and government-business relationships have contributed to the country's expansion, some feel that the main driving forces behind this growth have been technological innovations and a social psychology and consciousness unique to Japan. Others explain Japan's success on the basis of some economic myths which have grown up as the criteria for Japan's industrial development.

In the first place, a common myth has been that Japan has "cheap" labor. It does have an industrious, educated labor force which is efficient and flexible, but labor is not "cheap". Its labor rates are much higher than in other parts of Asia and, in some of its major industries, are comparable to those of Western Europe. Secondly, it has been assumed by many that Japan "exports to live." Actually, Japan exports only ten to twelve percent of its total output which is much less than most industrialized countries. Japan's exports are important because of the need for foreign exchange to import food and raw materials, but its production is primarily for the domestic market to meet the demands of its 100 million people. A third myth is that the Japanese are copiers, unable to produce original products or ideas. In actual practice, Japanese industry invests substantially in research and development with excellent results which are beginning to take the form of licenses from Japanese companies to foreign firms. It is true, however, that much of Japan's innovations in technology have been built upon a western base. Its management practices and philosophy, on the other hand, are more unique to Japan and differ in several respects from those of Europe and the United States.

Other countries throughout the world during the last two decades (1950-70) have had opportunities to receive technology from the industrialized nations, but have not assimilated this technology and built upon it the way Japan has. Two distinct human and social (rather than strictly economic) characteristics of the Japanese culture have contributed to the country's ability to use effectively technological innovations. These characteristics are (1) <u>shudan ishiki</u> or "group spirit," and (2) a restless vitality and desire to be active.

<u>Shudan ishiki</u> is a way of thinking which emphasizes group rather than individual interest and development. Through identification and a sense of belonging to a group, changes in ways of doing things create fewer anxieties on the part of the individual. Illustrative of this sense of identification is that frequently a Japanese will respond to the question of what he does for a living with the name of the company by which he is employed, not with his position (salesman, engineer, or accountant) within the company. Sometimes, in responding to foreigners, he may think of himself as part of a broader group comprising his industry, the government, and the financial institutions.

Related to this group spirit is a desire to work together to help the enterprise become larger. This emphasis for expansion is part of the continuing policy of absorbing new technology, investing in new equipment, and providing opportunities for employees to advance rapidly within the organization. With this greater emphasis on growth rather than profits, equity capital accumulation has been negligible with the result that Japanese companies have one of the lowest equity to debt ratios among industrialized nations.[7]

EMPLOYEE RELATIONS

A group spirit is also stimulated by the fact that Japanese managements' practices have included the system of lifetime employment, seniority, and a wage structure somewhat related to the concept of an enterprise as a family. Since the future of all employees depends upon the success of the company under such personnel policies, management and employees have cooperated in achieving goals of growth and development.

The lifetime employment system (shushin koyo) which developed out of custom and tradition was institutionalized fully only after World War II. It therefore represents a somewhat recent policy in Japanese business. Not all firms in Japan are sufficiently large to insure lifetime employment. Also, not all employees, particularly women, are considered permanent workers eligible for tenure. Other nontenured employees exist in such industries as shipbuilding and large steel companies where 25 to 30 percent or more of the total work force may be employees of a subcontractor. In these industries, certain production processes, transportation and loading, repair and maintenance, and other functions may be subcontracted to small labor-intensive firms, thereby providing greater flexibility in the work force.[8]

Another kind of flexibility existing in the work force is the retirement system employed by many Japanese companies. Although the retirement age is 55, selected executives and employees are retained beyond this age for important positions in management or the labor force. Because of the security offered by lifetime employment, workers and management are willing to effect changes for the benefit of the company. Anyone leaving to join a different company cannot gain in the new company the seniority and lifetime employment security he had with his initial employer, with the result that most employees tend to stay with the company which hired them upon graduation from high school or college.

Seniority (nenko joretsu), or merit of years, represents the devotion of the employee to the company as measured by years of service. Promotion and wages are related to length of service, which is also a factor of age and education, as permanent or regular employees typically join the Japanese company upon graduation.

Prior to World War II, promotion into the higher ranks of management was influenced by kinship to a particular family or political partisanship, whereas in the postwar period much more attention has been given to competence. However, such competence is evaluated not according to standards of management as a universal "profession" which is transferable from one company to another but according to the needs of the company and the value of the individual to the company as he has progressed up through the ranks.[9] Up to and including middle management, seniority remains the major criteria for advancement with the result that much attention is devoted to the training and placing of each person in the type of position where the enterprise as a whole can expect the best contribution from each.

Salaries and wages, particularly in the larger firms, include many fringe benefits such as bonuses, allowances for children, transportation, housing, entertainment, leisure, and medical expenses. In effect, because of the lifelong employment and seniority system, Japanese wages and salaries might be considered as a guaranteed life insurance paid in installments depending upon the living and social needs of the individual. Additional benefits including welfare facilities such as company housing, summer camps, and recreation facilities represent an added cost of labor which does not appear in the salary figures. Severance pay on retirement also adds to wage costs amounting to as much as three or four years' salary. The semiannual bonus payments of most companies in June and December varies from 25 percent to 60 percent or more of the employee's annual salary, depending upon the business and profitability of the company. Consequently, Japan's wages, including fringe benefits, are presently at European levels.

In Japan, wages in general are a matter of length of service rather than the job which the individual performs. Entering salaries are based upon years of education and the quality of the schools or university which the person attended. Merit and position increases based upon performance and ability begin after several years employment and it is from this time to age forty that the salaries of the average employee reflect a combination of seniority and performance. Since the salary of a person in a relatively low position increases each year regardless of performance, a young person with greater ability may receive a lower salary for the same work. Eventually, if Japan is to continue its progress toward being the leading industrial nation in the world, some changes will have to be made to place emphasis on the employee's ability to contribute to the goals and objectives of the company rather than on age and length of service.

In small enterprises, which make up 90 percent of the companies and employ half the labor force, little security exists for the worker. These small firms are not expected to become large and may succeed or fail depending upon the quality of management. Many, however, become associated with larger firms in a kind of parent-child relationship in which case they may exchange management and technical talent. Usually the former managers of the parent firm serve on the board of the child firm which may be a subcontractor. Although some large Japanese firms prefer to expand through their own resources, many believe that this so-called parent-child system provides more flexibility.

Just as the worker is rewarded more for his company affiliation than his skill or performance on a particular job, labor unions also are on a company basis in Japan. In fact, the Japanese labor union includes all the employees of the company up to section chiefs. In collective bargaining the unions concern themselves with the lifelong employment arrangements and pay. Employment regulations and welfare programs are considered the prerogative of management. Since the union as well as the employee is identified with the company rather than any craft or special interest groups, unions do not, in general, obstruct changes of jobs, retraining, nor transfers of its members, nor do they object to automation since these are "good" for the growth of the company and, therefore, "good" for the union. In some industries in which the employees are organized more on the basis of crafts and skills, one may encounter some resistance to change.

Japan does have industry-wide national labor unions whose membership is made up of the various company unions. The national headquarters of these unions are continually trying to gain more control over their strong, independent company-union members. Each spring the largest national labor organization in Japan, Sohyo, takes the lead in demanding higher wages for members of the government workers' unions which it represents. The actual wage negotiations and agreements are made by the company unions but the national, industry-wide unions try to influence the company unions not to make individual settlements. Wage increases have been granted year after year in most settlements but, since wages were low to begin with, these increases have not been a heavy burden on the individual companies nor the economy and, in most instances, have been offset by increases in productivity. [10]

FOREIGN TECHNOLOGY

In fact, a major factor contributing to Japan's rapid economic development since World War II has been its ability to increase productivity through the use of foreign technology. From 1950 to 1968, nearly 10,000 agreements were entered into for purchase of foreign technology in the form of patents, know-how, special studies, and reports at a total cost of approximately $1.5 billion.[11] The United States has been the principal source of this technology, primarily through licensing agreements and the payment of royalties usually at a rate of four or five percent. Japan has made it a practice to improve on the technology it has purchased and to develop its own products and processes.

The Ministry of International Trade and Industry (MITI) maintains control over the import of technology in accordance with its determination of needs and the development of Japanese technology in the various private and governmental research institutes. Foreign exchange controls have helped control competition among Japanese companies in the purchase of technology and the selection of the best available at a reasonable price. For example, if several firms are competing for foreign technology in such a way that production will far exceed demand, the Ministry of International Trade and Industry will try to persuade the companies to reach a compromise and, if this is not possible, MITI will make the decision.[12] Apparently, Japanese business considers MITI's decisions reasonable as they are made only after careful consultation and evaluation by committees on which industry is represented. In addition to reviewing agreements, the Japanese government also attempts to limit the duration of the agreements with the result that when the agreement terminates the foreign seller of the technology may find himself competing with the Japanese company without the receipt of royalties. Consequently, there is a tendency for foreign sellers of technology to Japan to insist upon some equity participation in the Japanese recipient in order to benefit from technological transfer over the long run. Joint ventures are also desirable because of the difficulty of enforcing any restrictive agreements with Japan for the export of products under license involving unpatentable know-how. Problems of this nature have led to growing reluctance of U.S. corporations to license technology to Japan, a situation which has caused some increased licensing from Europe.

In the future, it is expected that Japan will continue to purchase technology but the emphasis may shift from basic production to distinctive technology such as designs and trade marks and environmental technology, particularly in the area of pollution control. From the production standpoint it is expected that Japan will tend to specialize in certain industries as far as export is concerned such as its current position of producing most of the radios, tape recorders, and even television sets for the U. S. market. Japan will also probably loosen its controls over the purchase of technology in those industries which are important for national development or for Japan's future growth in the world markets. Through a combination of strategies reached by the industrial committees of the Ministry of International Trade and Industry, and its public and private research efforts, Japan should reach a position of technical competence equal to or exceeding that of other industrialized nations.

The economic development of Japan represents, therefore, a governmentally led, cooperative effort between small and big business, between government and industry, and between labor and management. Concurrent with this, Japanese corporations have continued to develop management practices and policies which have resulted in rapid growth not only of the company itself but of the Japanese economy as a whole.

NOTES

1. For a detailed description of the development of these associations see Yujiro Shinoda, Japan's Management Associations, Bulletin no. 15, (Tokyo: Sophia University Socio-Economic Institute, 1967).
2. Francis T. Vaughn, Joint Venturing in Japan, Bulletin no. 30, (Tokyo: Sophia University Socio-Economic Institute, 1971): 4-5.
3. Robert J. Ballon, Top Executives and Company Presidents in Japan, I. Function and Personality, Bulletin no. 27, (Tokyo: Sophia University Socio-Economic Institute, 1971): 16.
4. Peter F. Drucker, "What We Can Learn from Japanese Management," Harvard Business Review, (March-April 1971): 111-13.
5. See James C. Abegglen, ed., "Japan, Incorporated; Government and Business as Partners," Business Strategies for Japan, Chapter Four, pp. 71-82.
6. Minoru Masuda, "The Present Situation and Future Course of Japan's Overseas Investment," Management Japan, vol. 6, no. 2 (1972): 24-25.
7. Haruo Suzuki, "Innovation and Integration in Japanese Management," Management Japan, vol. 3, no. 3 (1969): 17, 21.
8. Akihisa Okada, Subcontracting Blue-Collar Workers (Case Study: The Nippon Steel Corporation, Nagoya Works), Bulletin no. 34, (Tokyo: Sophia University Socio-Economic Institute, 1972).
9. Robert J. Ballon, Top Executives and Company Presidents in Japan, I. Function and Personality, Bulletin no. 27, (Tokyo: Sophia University Socio-Economic Institute, 1971): 6.
10. Takao Nagata, "Japan's Labor-Management Relations," Management Japan, vol. 3, no. 2 (1969): 26.
11. James C. Abegglen, op. cit., p. 121.
12. Naohiro Amaya, The Ministry of International Trade and Industry, Bulletin no. 24, (Tokyo: Sophia University Socio-Economic Institute, 1970): 7.

CHAPTER 4

MANAGEMENT DEVELOPMENT

Most of the present top management of Japan is made up of men who were born in the Meiji era and graduated from college in the 1920s or early 1930s and were part of middle management during the 1940s. In a 1966 survey of presidents of 1,150 major companies listed in the Tokyo Stock Exchange[1] it was found that 88 percent had attended universities and approximately 27 percent were graduates of Tokyo University. Other public universities such as Kyoto, Hitotsubashi, Kobe and Tokyo Technical accounted for another 30 percent and 13 percent were graduates of Keio and Waseda Universities, both of which are private. One of the major forces contributing to Japan's remarkable progress under its present management is that higher education has been available to men of ability regardless of social background.

Only graduates from secondary schools of the highest quality are usually successful in passing satisfactorily the entrance examinations of the most prestigious universities. In most cases, the universities to which a graduate is eligible to apply may depend upon the type of secondary school which he attended. If the student has attended a "poor" secondary school, his situation is more difficult. The "best" universities may admit only one out of ten or more who take the final entrance examinations. Under these circumstances, those who can afford tutoring sometimes have a better chance of admission. As in most countries, a large donation to a private university also enhances the applicant's position. In some of the larger universities, some nepotism and favoritism result in exceptions to selection on the basis of rigid entrance examinations alone. In general, however, the opportunity to enter a university or technical school combined with policies of promotion based upon education, seniority, and contribution to the organization has been instrumental in stimulating a desire on the part of young people to obtain a higher education in Japan. As income levels have increased within the country, more and more young people have applied to universities for higher education.

Japanese universities have traditionally emphasized philosophical thinking and training in theoretical principles rather than technical and practical education and training in specific subjects. Up until very recently, graduates of professional schools such as engineering were regarded merely as technicians who lacked the broad educational qualifications for management. As a result, most of the more than 100,000 new university graduates who enter Japanese industry each year are not specialists, but have a general education with a potential to be trained to become managers. Experts in technical knowledge and skills are generally recruited by industry from the lower-level technical schools. University graduates, therefore, who have been hired for eventual managerial positions, have had to learn technical skills through the company's own training facilities, combined with some outside training in various specialized educational centers which have been established in Japan during the past fifteen years.

Usually, technical education and training in specific functions is the responsibility of the technical experts in the departments in which the new graduate works. Graduates are transferred between various functions within the enterprise in order to get direct experience in various managerial areas and to develop their knowledge and skills so that they can assume positions requiring a broad general background of knowledge and experience. Technical education, therefore, within the company and by outside training institutions is given to young prospective managers as a part of preparing them for generalized management positions and not as a means of making them better technicians.

Because of the broad background which young management candidates have received as part of their formal education, they are usually quite capable of applying principles of systematic thinking to the solution of managerial problems and are well qualified to analyze and solve these problems. Within the framework of the general sociocultural background of the country, they gain a realistic, practical understanding of the business world through the day-to-day technical training which they receive within the company. When this is combined with their broader educational background, they acquire an ability to think theoretically and practically at the same time. The division of labor between the managerial staff and technical experts in Japanese industry is closely interwoven with the traditional policies of lifetime employment and the seniority system.

Since managerial personnel tend to remain for a lifetime of employment with the same company, young graduates seek a company affiliation where they feel opportunities exist for the development of their potential. Similarly, a company's growth and diversification is dependent upon the quality of its managerial personnel.

A university graduate, therefore, choses a job primarily upon the basis of the reputation of the company rather than on the nature of the starting position itself. The large companies attract some of the best talent. These companies continually recruit at the highly rated universities which present candidates for the companies entrance examinations. Candidates are required to present information concerning their academic performance, experience, their family and names of people they know in the company who might sponsor them. For these large companies, as few as ten percent of the candidates pass the entrance examinations and are admitted to the corporation for lifetime employment.

Once a young man has entered the employ of the business organization, he generally finds there are two kinds of systems existing within the company which have an effect upon his progress and development. First, there is the status system which emphasizes seniority and lifetime employment; and second, there is the task system which emphasizes the functional assignments to competent persons without regard to their formal status within the organization. Both of these systems operate quite informally within the company, but they do exist. These systems are based somewhat upon the traditional family system whereby each member is given a certain amount of protection and security and at the same time is assigned those tasks which are most appropriate for him to perform. Management development in Japan, therefore, has occurred within the traditional framework of the family social structure which has become part also of the philosophy and the thinking of the corporate structure. Management education and training recognizes this customary division of labor.

Revolutionary changes in technology have created a problem of trying to achieve a balance between the generalist's technical knowledge and his overall broader educational needs. Traditionally, technical education in management was primarily concerned with keeping abreast with the progress in changes in management science. However, changes in technology have made it necessary for more and more managers to have a fundamental knowledge of many principles that exist in scientific areas outside of management alone. The new demands for technical education in business have had an influence on Japanese universities which currently are attempting to cope with these recent developments in technological sciences within the framework of their traditional academic approach which emphasizes the study of philosophy and the classical sciences. The demands for this technical education have been met partly by university level education and to some extent by industry-wide educational training programs which have gone into effect with the cooperation of universities and other institutions which organize industrial and management education and training. Technical training has been given mainly to the junior and middle classes of management staffs. With regard to top level management, well qualified technical experts generally have been assigned as members of their staff to keep them abreast of changes and help them adapt to the technical needs of the corporation.

Actually, the impact of the technical training in Japanese industrialization has created some changes in the value system of Japanese culture; particularly among the younger generations. Those who have been educated in the university system of the 1950s and 60s have been indoctrinated with the philosophies of western democracy. Consequently, their concepts and attitudes toward the traditional seniority system and philosophy of lifetime employment have tended to change. As a result, the seniority system has been gradually losing its social significance in the past twenty years. Technological progress has tended to create situations in which young men entering the company may be more useful than those with greater seniority. Competition among companies for outstanding technical and managerial personnel is beginning to weaken some of the advantages of seniority and lifetime employment. In fact, in order to remain competitive, Japanese companies have found it necessary to add performance evaluation to their personnel practices in order to place emphasis on ability rather than on length of service and age alone.[2]

Management development in the Japanese company, on the other hand, is determined more by the needs of the organization and society than by the needs of the individual. Under these circumstances, a person's responsibilities are less clearly defined and his general advancement is determined more by experience than educational background, and by continuing education as such. As a result, individual competence becomes recognized as the person moves from one position to another and as he participates in in-company training programs.

Among young people, new concepts of democracy and individualism are beginning to take root. Education in Japan, traditionally, was made up of highly systematized series of courses which each person took. With the expansion of television, which was in 96.3 percent of the Japanese homes in 1968, and with the increase of magazine sales and distribution, children and young people in Japan have been introduced to complex social phenomena which they interpret in their own manner in such a way that they do not accept as readily the traditional institutionalized education. This attitude combined with rapid technological change has tended to widen the generation gap in Japan and has made young people more individualistic, selfish, and impulsive. Companies, therefore, and the educational system itself have found it necessary to place more emphasis on individualism and the introduction of western management practices with the resulting increases in training both within and outside the company.

In 1970, the Tokyo Chamber of Commerce published the results of a survey of 683 company presidents regarding the development of personnel for top management positions.[3] Most of the companies had no systematic in-house training but relied upon outside top management seminars. More than eighty percent of the company presidents surveyed stated that graduate schools of business were needed in Japan. However, such an expressed need for graduate business education would be difficult to measure in practical terms since MBA degree programs in Japan were practically nonexistent in 1970. Some of them felt a need for formal graduate education which might have been an outgrowth of top management seminars conducted by Japanese universities.

UNIVERSITY PROGRAMS

At this university level, western top management concepts were introduced at Keio University in 1956 at which time the Keio-Harvard Advanced Management Program was inaugurated.[4] Initially, members of the faculty of the Harvard Business School in the United States came to Japan as instructors in this program which offered Japanese managers an opportunity to acquire the most advanced knowledge and information concerning American management practices and techniques, to develop skills in understanding management problems from the top management point of view, and to implement practical decisions. It is a one-year residential program for high level managers and is customarily held at a resort hotel in Japan. The Keio University Business School offers a two-week management development seminar for middle managers and a four-week in-resident program of a similar nature for junior managers. The case method of instruction is used in all of these programs and the faculty consists of Harvard-trained Japanese professors supplemented at times with visiting United States faculty from the Harvard Business School. In 1969, the Business School of Keio University inaugurated a two-year MBA program patterned after that offered by the Harvard Business School which, through the use of the case method, combines the qualitative and quantitative approaches in order to develop potential managers capable of applying both techniques effectively for decision-making.

The International Division of the School of Business of Sophia University also began a Master's program in International Business and Management in 1967. This program is conducted in English and focuses its attention especially upon the young Japanese executive who wishes to develop into an international businessman. Case studies are used combined with management theory. The orientation is on international management as viewed from Japan. Sophia University also has an undergraduate school of business administration.

Supplementing Sophia University's Master's program are the International Management Development Seminars offered by its Socio-Economic Institute. These seminars are usually two or three days in duration and are conducted by members of the faculty of the university and visiting lecturers from business and other universities. A wide range of topics has been offered in subjects relating to finance, personnel, marketing, governmental relations, and joint ventures, including a special workshop for foreign executives' wives. Under the leadership of Professor Robert J. Ballon, Sophia University's Socio-Economic Institute is known worldwide for its research and publications on Japanese business and personnel management. Its publications, which are in English, include such books as <u>Doing Business in Japan</u>, <u>The Japanese Employee</u>, and <u>Joint Ventures and Japan</u>. Each year it publishes, in English, a number of monographs on a variety of topics relating to Japanese business.

In addition to their graduate schools and top management seminars, both Sophia University and Keio University have undergraduate schools of business administration. Another educational organization which offers undergraduate instruction in business administration topics is the Institute of Business Administration and Management (IBAM). This institute was founded in 1950 as an outgrowth of the Japanese Efficiency School, originally established by Yoichi Uyeno in 1942 to conduct courses in the areas of efficiency, office management, cost accounting, work study, personnel management, and production control. These were conducted as evening courses and when the Institute was established in 1950, it continued to offer evening courses as well as day sessions. Although the academic portion of the institute is primarily a junior college and a correspondence school, it is recognized as a leading training center for young executives both from Japanese and U.S. joint venture companies. In 1964, the Institute was instrumental in introducing the techniques of Management by Results which was initially put into practice by such organizations as the Sumitomo Bank, Toshiba Electric Company and the Japan Telephone and Telecommunication Company. The following year, IBAM began a series of courses on the Managerial Grid. As a result, the Institute has become one of the leaders in offering sensitivity training, management grid seminars, computer utilization, and subjects of this nature in addition to the more than twenty-five diversified management courses which are offered to junior managers in business and government on a part-time basis.

In 1969, a graduate-level training organization, the Institute for International Studies and Training was established and is one of the most important for government officials, businessmen, and others who have careers in international affairs. This Institute operates under the general supervision of the Japanese Ministry of International

Trade and Industry with a board of directors representing government, business, and educational institutions. It was initially financed by a $10,000,000 grant made up of contributions from government and business. Its campus located near Mt. Fuji was completed in 1970 and includes living quarters, faculty housing, classrooms, a library and the like. Its one-year course with an enrollment of 120 is the main program offered by the Institute. The course includes an intensive study of English plus one other foreign language, area studies of selected countries, international business, and a one-week tour of Japan plus one month abroad in the selected area of concentration. Twenty-five full-time faculty are in resident at the Institute and their instruction is supplemented by guest lecturers and seminar leaders who are brought to the campus each year.

OTHER MANAGEMENT DEVELOPMENT PROGRAMS

In addition to the Institute and formal university academic programs at both the graduate and undergraduate levels and the university sponsored management seminars, Japanese consulting firms, productivity centers, and other organizations offer a variety of other training programs in top management and the various functional areas of business administration. A number of these training programs are conducted by the Japan Management Association which is a nonprofit association of management consultants and is the largest in the country. The courses of the Management Association are usually offered at the organization's headquarters in Tokyo. Although, generally not considered as residential programs, they are typically of one to two weeks duration on a full-time basis. Among courses offered by the Japan Management Association are those which were begun in the 1950s and which deal with problems of industrial engineering and related functions, such as, production control, preventive maintenance, and inventory control. These courses are offered to middle managers in the production departments of manufacturing enterprises and are conducted three to six times a year depending upon the demand. The teaching faculty in these courses is made up of consultants who are members of the Japan Management Association. In the 1960s the Japan Management Association began to offer courses in other functional areas such as, market research applications, sales management, and office management. These programs, likewise, typically of one week duration, are taught by the Japan Management Association consultants and the participants are usually managers in the respective area of specialization in which the course is offered.

In 1955, the Nippon Electric Company introduced the Zero Defects program (ZD) as a part of its quality control. The following year, the Japan Management Association sent a study team to the United States to study the program and established a ZD Promotion Center which eventually lead to the adoption of the ZD movement by 7,000 companies in various industries covering a total of five million employees.[5] In 1966, the Japan Management Association inaugurated a top management course of eight days duration which is conducted twice a year. This course is open to senior executives and is designed to provide a fundamental knowledge of the nature of management including the significance of technology, marketing, organizational structures, human relations, and management rationalization. The faculty consists of a director and two other full-time staff members of the Japan Management Association. The case method is used primarily with materials which have been prepared by the Japan Management Association. Typically, the person attending this course is an executive director of an operating division in his company.

The Japan Productivity Center, established in 1954 in cooperation with the United States Government, offers a variety of training programs throughout Japan in its area branches and also at its headquarters in Tokyo. The courses at the managerial level include managerial economics, decision-making and management information, personnel administration and industrial relations, human resource development, and top management. The managerial economics course is of forty-five days duration on a part-time basis. It is offered one full day a week for ten months and is typically attended by middle managers from general management, research departments, systems departments, and allied areas, mostly from large industrial companies. This program is based primarily upon lectures and its faculty consists of professors of accredited universities in the Tokyo area. Other courses are fifty weeks in duration and are part-time programs offered either on the basis of one evening or one half-day a week for a year. The top management course is conducted one morning a week for a year and is typically attended by senior executives in various functional areas of management, such as, directors, division chiefs, plant managers, or, in smaller companies, presidents or vice presidents. This course is limited to executives in industry and men from government or the service professions.

In 1965, the Academy of Management Development was established as part of the Japan Productivity Center. The purpose of the Academy was to introduce the modern management and business administration techniques of the United States and Western Europe into Japan. The Academy offers nine programs in each of the major functional areas of management such as marketing, production, finance, systems, and computers. All these programs offer the participants a systematic understanding of the latest scientific theories

and their applications to their respective functional areas. Most of
these courses are conducted for one day a week over a lengthy period
of time such as a year. The Academy has a full-time dean who is
assisted by four or more senior university professors from the Tokyo
area who take charge of various courses and teach in the sessions.
Typically, the participants in the program are junior managers in
their respective functional areas. The Japan Productivity Center
with its Academy of Management Development is the largest management training organization in Japan and has centers located throughout
the country.

In 1961, the Asian Productivity Organization was established
with its headquarters in Japan for the purpose of accelerating the
economic development of countries in the Far East. Its membership
consists of the Republic of China, Hong Kong, India, Ceylon, Indonesia,
Iran, Japan, Republic of Korea, Nepal, Pakistan, the Philippines,
Thailand, and Vietnam. The Asian Productivity Organization has developed some training programs and courses which it conducts through
the medium of the National Productivity Organizations of the respective
member countries. With its headquarters in Japan, the Asian Productivity Organization conducts once a year a twenty-four week residential
program called Small Business Management Trainers and Consultants
Training Course. Twenty weeks are spent in Japan and four in one of
the other member countries where the participants have an opportunity
to observe the technical application of their instruction. Typically,
the participants from the other member countries are managers, consultants or accountants, and government specialists. Another twelve-week residential program in Tokyo conducted by the Asian Productivity
Organization is the Production-Level Engineers Training Course.
This is made up of a combination of classroom instruction, observational plant visits and on-the-job training in factories in the vicinity
of Tokyo. The faculty for this program are typically business executives in the Tokyo area.

Other Japanese Management training programs include those of
the Japan Institute of Business Administration (JIBA), the Central
Japan Institute of Industrial Management in Nagoya, Japan, and the
Japanese Standards Association. The latter, established in 1945, is
a private organization under government sponsorship with the support
of industry and works on matters of industrial standardization. Its
Quality Control and Standardization Seminar is a twenty-five day
course for middle managers in manufacturing and quality control and
is given on a full-time basis in each of seven major cities once or
twice a year. The Central Japan Institute of Industrial Management
is an affiliate of the Central Japan Industries Association established
in 1953 to offer management consulting services to its members.
The Institute's Junior Executive Academy is a one-year full-time

course given in Nagoya for young men who are to be successors to top management in family businesses. Approximately 40 percent of the program is devoted to a study of in-plant practices including those of the company for which the junior executive is being trained. The instructors are members of the management consulting firm supplemented by outside guest speakers from industry. The Management Development program of the Japan Institute of Business Administration is a ten-month part-time course for middle and senior managers in personnel training, labor relations and general management. The program was started in 1968 as a division of the Japan Management School, a nonprofit management education correspondence school and one of the largest among many schools of this type in Japan. The director of the program and its instructors are senior professors at the University of Tokyo and other major universities in the Tokyo area.

IN-COMPANY TRAINING

For Japanese industry, however, the major training efforts are those within the company itself. The larger companies all have comprehensive training programs for the development of their managerial and technical personnel. One of the most outstanding company training centers is that of the Hitachi Company which was completed in 1962. It is a spacious center patterned somewhat after the training center of General Electric in Crotonville, N.Y. It is solely a resident training facility for top management and its curriculum includes not only managerial topics but also such typically Japanese subjects as the composition of poetry.[6]

Illustrative of a comprehensive training program for administrative and technical personnel is that of the Toyota Motor Company. (See Charts 2 and 3.) As noted in the outlines, Toyota's program and system training is a combination of on-the-job instruction by supervisors and technicians and formal lectures and courses for all levels of employees from workers to top management. Toyota's training system reflects the international character of its operations. In addition, as indicated in Chart 2, the sales department is a separate and independent company under two top managers who work closely together in guiding the two entities. The Toyota training program for the production operations is similar to that of other companies in Japan. As illustrated in Chart 4, Toshiba's training program includes similar subject matter and training courses for its administration and technical personnel at all levels. Companies in Japan are continually upgrading personnel through formal training courses and on-the-job experiences in order to strengthen the various operations. Training

CHART 2

Toyota Motor's Training System

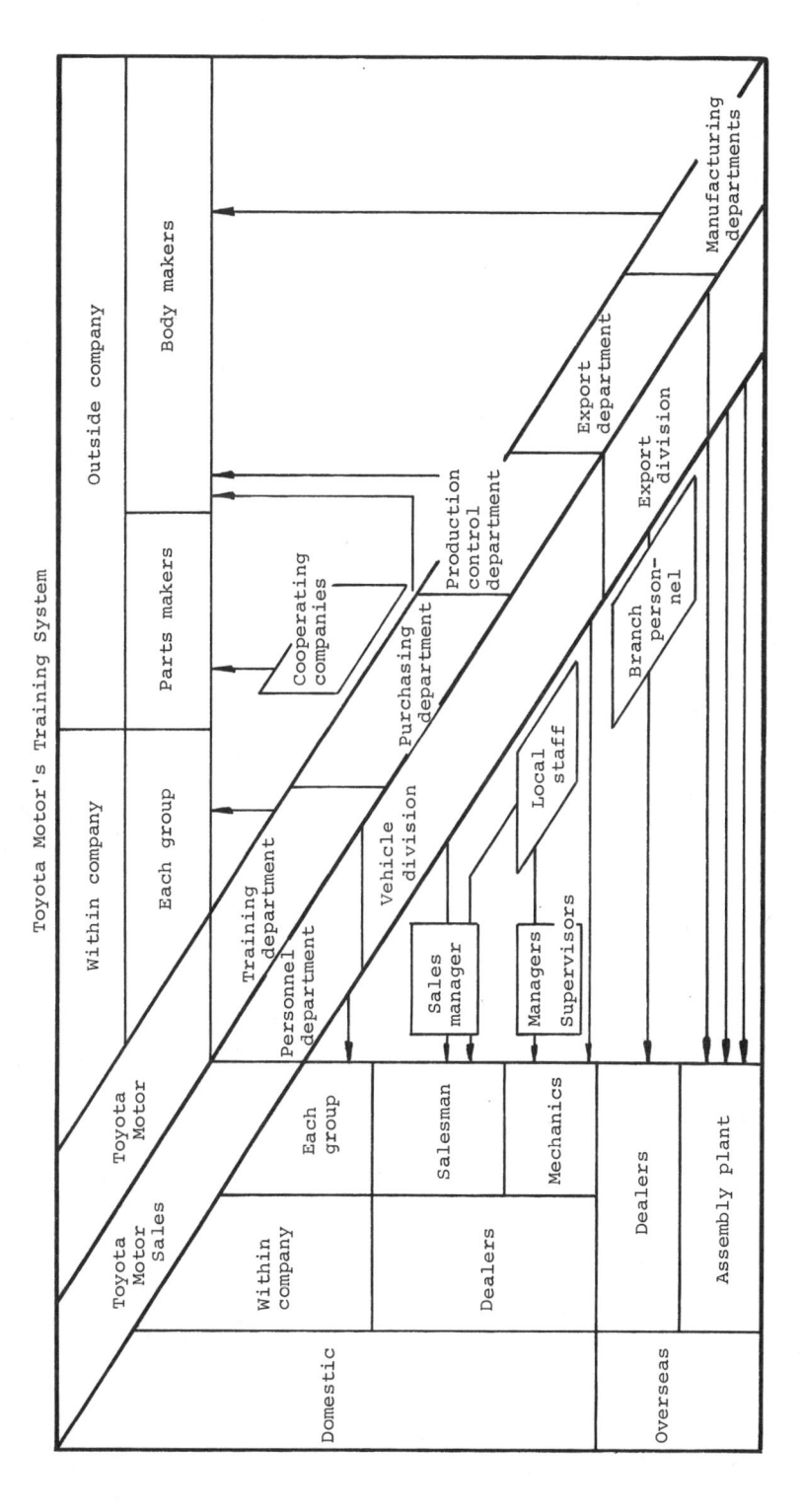

Source: Gen Numaguchi, "Toyota Motors' Management Policy and World-Wide Strategy," *Management Japan*, vol. 3, no. 1 (1969), p. 27.

CHART 3

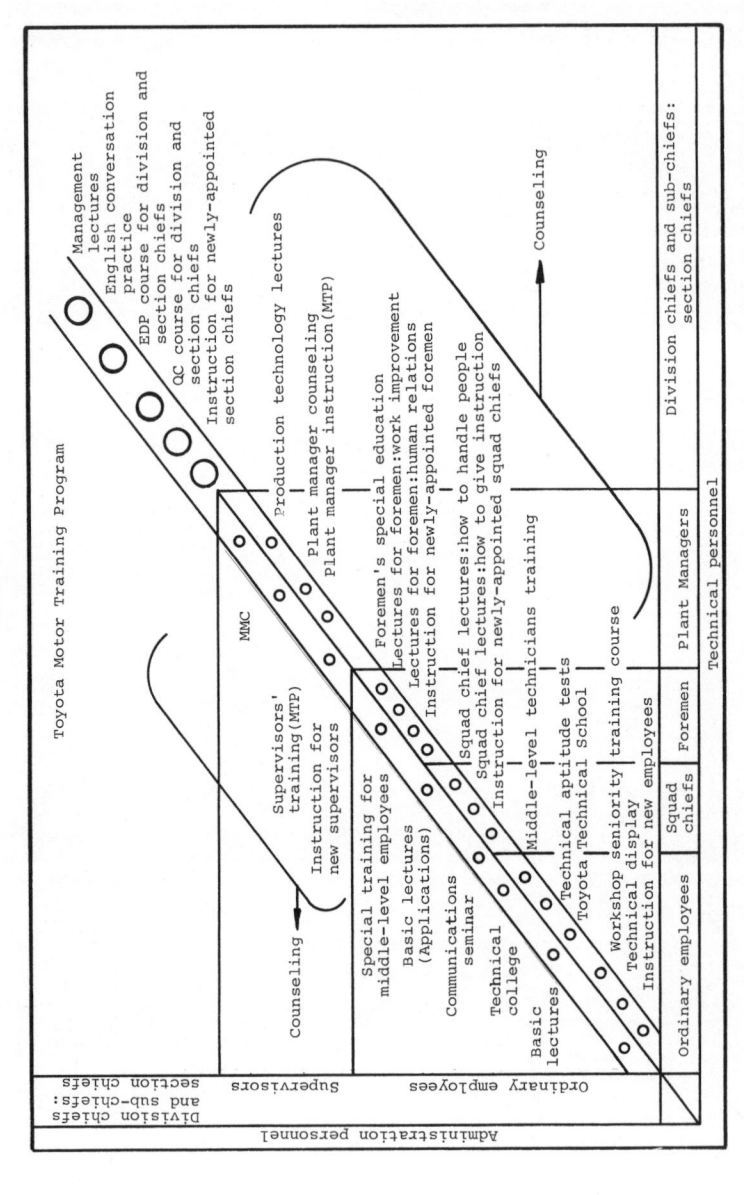

Toyota Motor Training Program

Administration personnel / Technical personnel

| Division chiefs and sub-chiefs: section chiefs | Supervisors | Ordinary employees | | Ordinary employees | Squad chiefs | Foremen | Plant Managers | Division chiefs and sub-chiefs: section chiefs |

Counseling

Supervisors' training (MTP)
Instruction for new supervisors

Special training for middle-level employees
Basic lectures (Applications)
Communications seminar
Technical college
Basic lectures

MMC

Middle-level technicians training
Technical aptitude tests
Toyota Technical School
Workshop seniority training course
Technical display
Instruction for new employees

Foremen's special education
Lectures for foremen: work improvement
Lectures for foremen: human relations
Instruction for newly-appointed foremen
Squad chief lectures: how to handle people
Squad chief lectures: how to give instruction
Instruction for newly-appointed squad chiefs

Production technology lectures
Plant manager counseling
Plant manager instruction (MTP)

Counseling

Management lectures
English conversation practice
EDP course for division and section chiefs
QC course for division and section chiefs
Instruction for newly-appointed section chiefs

Source: Nobuo Noda, How Japan Absorbed American Management Methods, Translation Series-10, "Asian Productivity Organization" (Tokyo, 1969), p. 37.

also includes the building of an esprit de corps and company loyalty. As Japanese companies have expanded overseas, they have taken with them the techniques and philosophy of their training activities in teaching the foreign nationals.

INTERNATIONAL MANAGEMENT TRAINING

In 1966, an International Management Cooperation Committee (IMCC) was established within the framework of the International Management Association of Japan to extend assistance to developing countries by sending Japanese Management Volunteer Executives (MVE) overseas. The IMCC is similar to the International Executive Service Corps (IESC) of the United States which was established in 1964 in response to a suggestion made by David Rockefeller in his keynote address at the 13th CIOS Congress in New York in September, 1963. During the first year of its operation IMCC sent two volunteer executives to Taiwan to give assistance to a Chinese company in accounting and design. In 1967, twenty-two executives were sent to such countries as Taiwan, Korea, and Colombia, South America. Assistance, in 1967, included production control, industrial design, labor-management relations, financial control, and marketing. Before leaving Japan, the volunteer executives make a thorough study of the operations, customs, technical level, and language of the countries to which they are going. The IMCC program has been enthusiastically received by the cooperating enterprises in the developing nations and has been extended to include 35 to 40 executives a year to the following countries in addition to those served in 1967: Pakistan, Peru, Brazil, Hong Kong, Ceylon, Thailand, and Ecuador.

The International Management Cooperation Committee is managed by 38 standing members and has 162 member companies which endorse its objectives and support it financially and by supplying personnel.[7] The Japanese government also gives financial assistance and moral support but does not impose any restrictions. The objectives of the Committee are to contribute to the industrial development and economic growth of developing countries by cooperating in the modernization and rationalization of management control in their enterprises. The IMCC sends volunteer executives only by invitation and, with the financial assistance of the members of the Committee and the Japanese government, the recipient organization need only pay a portion of the volunteer's maintenance expenses. As a general rule, assistance is given for a two to three month period. Although it is difficult to give much pertinent guidance in such a short period of time, the volunteers cannot spare too much time since they are actively engaged in managerial activities within their respective companies. This feature is

CHART 4

Toshiba's Training Program

		ADMINISTRATIVE		
		On-the-job training		Off-the-job instructional
Training Program	All employees group training	Plant or division group training	Division and section group training	On-the-job training
Division chiefs training program		Lectures, discussions, section chief round-table discussions	Study group in each division	Organization for on-the-job training on the basis of management for results
Section chiefs training program	Section chiefs training lectures (labor divisions)			
Managers training program		MTP follow up (case studies), managers training lectures, responsibility lectures, managers round-table discussion	Managers study group: responsibility training	Division delegation of responsibility, goal determination and transfer of authority, training re: goal determination time, control pertinent to achievement of goals, evaluation of training results
Management essentials training program		MTP management essentials lectures, responsibility lectures, TWI short course	Work-site study group (rotation of discussion leaders, discussions)	
Special responsibility training program	Attendant at vocational school (labor divisions): specialized responsibility lectures (head office, staff level)	Specialized responsibility lectures	Study groups in each division and section (rotation of discussion leaders, discussion)	Meetings, rotation of assignments, temporary substitution assignments, determination of study topics, complementing application of group training
Newly-hired college graduate training program	Commercial and plant practice: introductory lectures (by personnel dept.)	Divisional group training lectures	Work-site instruction meetings	
Newly-hired high school graduate training program		Introductory lectures (by personnel dept.), basic practices training, observation and instruction	On-the-job training	Skills evaluation, preparation for testing

SPECIALIZED VOCATIONAL TRAINING PROGRAMS / Managerial Training Programs

GENERAL ADMINISTRATIVE AND TECHNICAL TRAINING PROGRAMS

training	TECHNICAL					
	off-the-job training				
	Division and section group training	Plant or division group training	All employees group training	SPECIALIZED VOCATIONAL TRAINING PROGRAMS — Managerial Training Programs / Training Program	GENERAL ADMINISTRATIVE AND TECHNICAL TRAINING PROGRAMS / Training Program
		Foremen training lectures, MTP short course, creative thinking course, foremen's study group	All foremen's group training	Foremen's training program	
Squad study groups, technical instruction		Supervisory fundamentals training lectures, squad chief training lecture, TWI(JR), squad chief technical lectures, squad chief round table discussions		Squad chief training program	
Work-site study groups, technical instruction		TWI(JI, JM), basic management lectures, basic technical lectures, WSTC		Middle-level technicians training program	
Work-site fundamentals practical application		Technical lectures, basic education lectures			General technicians training program
Working on the job		High school graduates technical training curriculum, junior high school graduate technicians (trainees) training curriculum			Technicians training program
		Introductory lectures, basic practices training, observation and instruction			Newly-hired high and junior high school graduates training program

Notes: a. MTP=Manpower Training Program; TWI=Training Within Industry; JR=Job Relation; JM=Job Method; WSTC=Work Simplification Training Course b. Training outside the company is not included in this table.

Source: Nobuo Noda, "How Japan Absorbed American Management Methods, Translation Series--10," Asian Productivity Organization"(Tokyo, 1969), p. 33.

in contrast to the International Executive Service Corps of the United States which recruits many of its volunteers from the ranks of retired personnel who are no longer active in their companies or organizations.

Supporting the International Management Cooperation Committee is only one of several ways in which the Japanese private sector is cooperating in the field of management development programs in the developing countries. In addition to this volunteer assistance overseas, Japan's Technical Training Centers are open to participants from other countries. Its industry and government support the Asian Productivity Organization and the latter's member technical training centers in the developing nations of Asia. Japan's Association for Overseas Technical Assistance was established in 1959 for the purpose of giving technical and general education to industrial trainees from developing countries in a combination academic and in-plant practical training program in private Japanese enterprises. In 1962, the Overseas Technical Cooperation Agency (OTCA) was formed to give technical assistance by sending experts overseas and setting up training centers in developing countries. One activity of this Agency has been to send teams of young experts to assist in raising productivity, particularly in the field of agriculture.

Direct overseas investments by Japanese enterprises have also resulted in the extension of in-plant training in management techniques to the local foreign nationals employed by the affiliate in the developing country. These investments as of December, 1971 numbered more than 3,000 with an aggregate value of $4.23 billion in 100 countries.[8] The characteristic features of Japan's foreign investments are that:
1. they are mostly in the developing nations of Asia and the Far East,
2. production is for the local market,
3. the scale of operation is small with a limited capital investment in each venture,
4. most are joint ventures,
5. Japan's share of the joint venture is frequently in the form of machinery and equipment produced in Japan and sent to the affiliate in the developing nation, and
6. management and technology are supplied from Japan.

The top management of the parent company in Japan as well as the Japanese executives in charge of local operations in these developing nations realize that these ventures cannot be solely for profit but that they are expected to contribute to the economic and industrial development of the emerging nation in which they are located.

The Japanese feel, however, that such contributions cannot be fully realized by a developing nation because of its slowness in the development of human resources. This situation leads to poor planning and administrative ability, bureaucratic inefficiency, low productivity, lack of managerial skill and entrepreneurship, and a shortage of technical personnel and skilled labor. Unless an emerging nation has a sound program of education and training for the development of human resources, the investment of capital and the introduction of modern techniques will not be effective in making a significant contribution to the overall economic growth of the country. The Japanese corporations expanding overseas are fully aware of these limitations and, therefore, include as part of their investment programs a carefully planned on-the-job training for the overseas national both in his native country and in Japan itself. Although initially Japanese corporations found it difficult to recruit local nationals in those countries which had been occupied by Japan during World War II, evidence of Japanese efficiency in production and marketing has attracted many highly capable young men to the Japanese companies overseas. Matsushita Electric Industrial Company's overseas management philosophy of meeting the needs of the developing nation by adapting to its economy and customs rather than forcing itself upon the local people is typical of the new business philosophy Japanese industry is following with regard to its overseas expansion.

In general, therefore, management development is important to the Japanese company both at home and abroad. Universities in Japan are gradually changing their teaching methods and curricula to meet more effectively the needs in industry. Graduate programs in management are beginning to be offered and it seems apparent that industry feels a need for and will support such programs. Although most large companies have their own in-house training for technical and supervisory skills, top and middle management training is done primarily by outside institutions such as universities, consulting firms, associations, and other private organizations. As Japan has continued its expansion overseas, companies have demonstrated increased interest and support of programs to train managers from emerging nations where Japanese investment is taking place. By tradition in its personnel policies Japanese industry has a strong commitment to education and management development, a condition which has helped contribute to the excellent progress which the country has made in economic and industrial development during the past hundred years.

NOTES

1. <u>Gendai Shacho No Shinjo Chosa</u> (Survey on the Background of Present-Day Presidents) (Bijinesu: July 1966).
2. See Hideo Inohara, <u>Personnel and Wage Administration for the Promotion of Efficiency (Case Study: Canon Co.)</u>, Bulletin no. 29, (Tokyo: Sophia University Socio-Economic Institute, 1971).

3. See Robert J. Ballon, Top Executives and Company Presidents in Japan, I. Function and Personality, Bulletin no. 27, (Tokyo: Sophia University Socio-Economic Institute, 1971): 7, 8.

4. For a detailed description of training programs and post-graduate education for management in Japan see McNulty, Nancy G. Training Managers, the International Guide.

5. For a detailed study of the development of ZD in Japan see Hideo Inohara, Importing Managerial Techniques (Case Study: the Zero Defects Movement) Bulletin no. 35 (Tokyo: Sophia University Socio-Economic Institute, 1972).

6. Nobuo Noda, How Japan Absorbed American Management Methods, p. 23.

7. See Shigeki Tashiro, "Roles and Activities of International Management Cooperation," Management Japan, vol. 3, no. 3 (1969): 32-35.

8. "New Trends in Japanese Investment," Management Japan, vol. 6, no. 1 (1972): 16.

CHAPTER 5

THE AMERICAN CORPORATION IN JAPAN

Just as Japanese companies have found it necessary to make changes in philosophy, policies, and procedures when operating overseas, the successful U.S. corporation in Japan has found it necessary to adapt its operations to affect a compromise between American and Japanese traditions. Japanese companies follow many policies which are quite different from those of American companies. One of the major differences is that of the decision-making process which is slow and difficult to pinpoint from the standpoint of who made the decision. In the Japanese organization the decision may be the result of a proposal generated at a lower level which when finally endorsed by the top is ready for immediate implementation throughout the entire organization. In an American organization the decision may be made promptly at the top but several weeks may be needed to motivate the people to accept the decision and put it into practice. Furthermore, with regard to decision-making, Japanese industry tends to place emphasis on consensus and the motivation of the entire organization. In the American corporation much more emphasis is placed on organizing the work to produce optimum results.[1]

Another difference which sometimes causes confusion in dealing with the Japanese is that authority and responsibility are not clearly defined in the Japanese organizational structure thereby making it difficult for the American businessman to determine exactly which person to deal with in making a decision. In fact, in Japan, there is no real individual authority as understood in American management. That authority which does exist stems from responsibility of a group for the performance of certain tasks. Usually the members of the group have been carefully selected and trained for directing, controlling, and performing tasks which have been assigned to them in accordance with a kind of harmony which regulates the whole enterprise.[2]

This harmonious approach to problems is in contrast to the American method of using reasoning and logic. Under such circumstances, the American businessman who has been trained to reason objectively becomes confused when he finds subjective considerations influencing decisions along with the facts in the situation.

An American firm entering into business in Japan, therefore, must be willing to make some compromise between the American and the Japanese philosophies and techniques of management. On the one extreme is the American philosophy which is based on the belief that individual rights and freedom are paramount and that each individual should be afforded the maximum opportunity for self development, with the result that the economic well-being of society, the community, and the organization is maximized through the maximization of individual human rights. Although the traditional Japanese philosophy and techniques of management are gradually changing toward a greater recognition of individual rights and freedom, Japanese operations are still primarily based on the belief that the interests of society, the group, and the organization are superior to the rights and freedom of the individual and economic well-being can only be maximized by subordinating the individual's interest and maximizing the interest of the group, the corporation, the community, or the country as a whole. The American corporations operating in Japan blend these two philosophies in the way in which their top management feels most appropriate for effective performance.[3] The extent to which compromises need to be made in management methods is also influenced by the type of business arrangement which the American company selects to undertake in Japan.

If the American company uses agents to distribute its products in Japan, no capital is involved and no problems arise with regard to hiring and supervising personnel. The disadvantages, however, are similar to those of using agents in any market in that the manufacturing company has little control over the distribution of the product, servicing is generally unsatisfactory, and, since the agent customarily handles many other products, promotion and intensive selling efforts are insufficient for the product to become firmly established in the Japanese market. For a period of time, Dupont used Japanese agents for marketing its products but found this kind of distribution unsatisfactory. Such agents did not regard Dupont as a permanent part of Japanese business and, therefore, followed policies and practices leading to short-term quick profits. In 1964, Dupont established its own offices in Japan, eliminating most of its agents by setting up a dealer organization over which it exercised strong control.

If the American company decides, however, to open a branch office in Japan, control over the distribution and sale of the product can be assured. With a branch office problems do arise concerning recruiting, selecting, and hiring personnel, finding suitable channels of distribution, gaining a knowledge of Japanese customs, and obtaining permission from the Bank of Japan to remit funds in and out of the country in accordance with its exchange controls. Recruiting one or two well qualified Japanese managers to represent the company in a branch office is less difficult than staffing a subsidiary or joint venture in Japan. The primary problem in finding one or two managers of this type is a matter of time. Because of the nature of the Japanese seniority, and lifetime employment traditions, well qualified prospective managers are not generally available in the job market looking for positions. Word must be passed through informal channels that a position is open, the candidate must be screened carefully with the assistance of Japanese whom the company can trust, and sufficient time must be allowed for the candidate to disengage himself honorably from the job he is holding. In this connection, if the foreign company is looking for an experienced man, he will probably already be employed and can best be approached through an intermediary to avoid embarrassment both to himself and his employer. The qualities of the candidate should be reviewed carefully in light of what characteristics are required for success in Japan and not necessarily those most appealing to an American such as ability to speak English, informality, and business aggressiveness. In addition, assistance from a knowledgeable Japanese friend should also be sought in evaluating the quality of the candidate's education and experience. Even though the candidate may be willing to change jobs to come to work for the foreign company's branch, he may encounter objections from his family and his current Japanese employer, with the result that considerable time may be required for the candidate to resolve all the problems connected with making the transfer. However, with patience and care, a foreign branch can secure qualified Japanese to head its operations.[4]

The majority of foreign operations in Japan are in the form of joint ventures. During the first three rounds of capital liberalization between July 1967 and September 1970, 524 lines of industry representing approximately 80 percent of the total lines of industry in Japan were permitted to have 50-100 percent foreign direct investment. However, of this total, only 77 were approved by the Japanese government for 100 percent ownership. The other 447 were permitted to have up to 50 percent of foreign participation.[5] Although a fourth round of liberalization issued in August 1971 permitted 100 percent ownership in more than 90 percent of the lines of industry in Japan, a joint venture has remained the most common type of foreign investment in Japan and the kind of operation for which American corporations must seek Japanese managerial counterparts.

The success of a joint venture with a Japanese company will depend upon the extent to which the foreign partner investigates the situation thoroughly before making a commitment and also takes into consideration differences in Japanese culture, language, traditions, business methods, social customs, government regulations, and personnel policies at each step in the process of establishing and operating the joint venture. The primary motive of the prospective Japanese partner to form a joint venture will probably be the acquisition of advanced technologies and brand names to meet competition. The American company, on the other hand, may be primarily interested in entering the Japanese market and perhaps using Japan as a base for its Far Eastern operations.

The first step in planning a joint venture,[6] therefore, is to make a comprehensive survey of the market potential in Japan and prospective Japanese partners. In making such a survey, it is best to work through foreign business consultants who specialize in joint ventures, trade associations, chambers of commerce, lawyers, bankers, accountants and others, many of whom have offices in the United States through which the American company can work in making the initial survey. In sending representatives to Japan to meet with prospective partners, it is important to select top management personnel as the Japanese are very conscious of titles of positions and tend to arrange interviews only with people of comparable rank. Sufficient time should be allowed to permit casual conversations and unhurried discussions. The Japanese discuss business more on a personal basis than through direct negotiation. Much general conversation and entertainment may preceed any discussion of business as the Japanese want to get to know the person and reach a position of mutual trust before discussing or negotiating a business agreement. Even when business is discussed the Japanese may not give direct answers or make immediate decisions. Another problem in negotiations as well as in the actual operation of the venture itself is that a Japanese, because of inbred politeness and consideration for others, rarely says "no," but may even say "yes" when he really means that he is listening and trying to understand. Furthermore, before making a decision, the Japanese partner may have to consult others such as his colleagues, trade associations, or government and explain to each what was said by both sides. The decision, therefore, is more a matter of consensus than a strictly negotiated agreement as such.

In spite of this, the American firm contemplating a joint venture should employ a reputable Japanese legal firm and possibly a local accountant to sit in on the discussions and negotiations. Both can be of valuable assistance in drawing up the type of agreement which would be acceptable to the Japanese partner. American companies place a great deal of faith in written documents and, therefore, attempt to prepare legal documents to cover all types of potential differencs and contingencies which might occur. For the Japanese, on the other hand, mutual trust between the parties is more important than the words of the contract so they prefer to sign a more general contract, get the venture going, and work out problems later as they occur.

With regard to negotiations, therefore, it is important that the American should be honest and frank with his prospective Japanese partner but he should not be dictatorial. By stating the situation clearly and reasonably he will generally gain the cooperation and understanding of the Japanese partner provided the latter feels that the American is well intentioned and seeking an agreement which will be for the benefit of both parties and not just for his own profit.[7]

With regard to dealings with the Japanese government, the American company will find it advantageous to let its Japanese partner handle the negotiations with the Ministry of International Trade and Industry. As long as the American and Japanese partner have a clear understanding of how they wish to work together, the close relationship between industry and government in Japan will result in a satisfactory agreement. The American partner, however, should insist that he be kept informed of what is happening and that no final commitments or decisions be made without his approval. In dealing with the government as with the Japanese partner, it is important that all aspects be clearly discussed and that the Ministry of International Trade and Industry be informed of all parts of the agreement between the parties in order to avoid difficulties at a later date.

Illustrative of varying motives for a joint venture and the selection of a Japanese partner is that of Caterpillar and Mitsubishi in 1963. One of the reasons that Mitsubishi gave for considering Caterpillar as a good partner was the value the latter attached to long and continued diligent service of its employees, a policy similar to that of Mitsubishi and other Japanese companies. In picking Shin Mitsubishi instead of the more experienced Komatsu which, at that time controlled 53 percent of the Japanese tractor market, Caterpillar respected Mitsubishi as a large diversified company and as a newcomer in the manufacture and sale of tractors. Mitsubishi, on the other hand, wished to expand its sale of its own tractors overseas through the utilization of Caterpillar's worldwide distribution organization and to gain advanced technology and management know-how from Caterpillar.[8]

The reaction of the top management of Komatsu to the threat of Caterpillar Mitsubishi competition was to initiate "Operation Almighty" in 1961 to close the gap between the quality of its machines when compared with the durability and trouble-free performance of Caterpillar under harsh environmental conditions. Operation "A" started with intensive training sessions from top management down through every level of management in manufacturing, staff departments, and sales. Komatsu's five-year schedule of training resulted in improved and new products including the development of underwater bulldozers, and expansion of its export market to Central and South America, Southeast Asia, the Middle East and Africa. As a result of its intensive training efforts, Komatsu was able to maintain its competitive position in Japan and increase its total sales worldwide by 400 percent between 1960-68.[9] Caterpillar Mitsubishi, likewise, has been comparably successful in increasing sales and in exporting its Japanese-made equipment outside of Japan through the Caterpillar distributors' network which has worked extremely smoothly because of mutual trust and understanding between the two partners in a joint venture which has eight to nine thousand employees.

Because of differences in motives, attitudes, and governmental objectives and policies, a long time may be required for the completion of an agreement which meets satisfactorily the goals of the American partner. For example, in 1964, at the time Texas Instruments applied to the Ministry of International Trade and Industry for permission to build a 100 percent owned plant for the production of integrated circuits, Texas Instruments was primarily interested in the Japanese market and a production facility for the Far East as an expansion in its manufacturing opreations in North America and Europe. Since the integrated circuit industry at that time had barely made a start in Japan, the Ministry of International Trade and Industry insisted on a joint venture with the investment ratio not exceeding 50 percent, a disclosure of patents, and confinement of production to a specific volume for three years from the inauguration of the joint venture.

Initially, Texas Instruments did not accept the conditions specified by Japan's Ministry of International Trade and Industry. However, by 1968, Fairchild and Motorola, also unable to make 100 percent investments in Japan, had established plants in Taiwan and South Korea and were exporting to Japan. Likewise, by this time, the Ministry of International Trade and Industry was favorably disposed toward a joint venture between Sony and Texas Instruments as the demand for integrated circuits had expanded to include not only computers but many other applictaions in office machines, radios, and tape recorders. Although companies like Hitachi, Tokyo Shibura Electric, and Mitsubishi Electric were also producing integrated circuits in Japan, it was felt that the joint efforts of Sony and Texas Instruments would result in a high quality product at a low price, thereby helping to reduce imports.[10] In 1968, compromises and modifications of thinking and objectives on both sides resulted in a highly successful joint venture, four years after negotiations were originally undertaken. Finally, in December, 1971, Texas Instruments was permitted to buy out Sony's share with the result that after seven years of negotiations and operations it had achieved its original objective of a wholly-owned subsidiary in Japan.

Matters of policy, staffing and labor relations can be problems for joint ventures and wholly-owned subsidiaries. Texas Instruments, however, maintained control over these matters even during the time it was on the basis of a 50-50 joint venture with Sony. It recruited both its managerial staff and employees in the open market rather than borrowing staff from its Japanese partner as many foreign companies do in their joint venture operations. Because Texas Instruments in Japan recruited and trained its own Japanese managers, it was able to operate even as a joint venture in Japan using a management style quite similar to that it employed in the United States and elsewhere in the world. In some matters of personnel policies regarding security and lifetime wages, it followed the Japanese practices, but modified these somewhat through the use of a merit system. Sony, initially in its Atsugi Plant and later throughout its organization, introduced many innovative management concepts in dealing with its employees. Shigeru Kobayashi, a Sony Managing Director in 1969 and the manager of its Atsugi Plant from 1961-69, has described his experiences in a book entitled Creative Management which has been translated into English.[11] In his book, Kobayashi refers from time to time to Texas Instruments and the importance which the latter attaches to the employee and the achievement of company goals by providing the kind of work environment which encourages the achievement of individual goals. Policies relating to managers defining their positions with constant review and revision to meet changing needs, the maintenance of an active flow of informal communications, work simplification, and philosophies of dealing with unions are some of the specific areas of the management thinking of Texas Instruments which Kobayashi mentioned as being related to and influencing his own management style at Sony. It is evident, therefore, that during the period of the Sony-Texas Instruments joint venture, managers on both sides maintained an attitude of adapting and combining Japanese and American management philosophy and techniques in such a way that the best of each was utilized as appropriate for their operations in Japan.

An integral part of the management style of Texas Instruments has been long-range planning, a technique to which its Japanese managers adapted well. In general, however, American firms place much more emphasis on long-range planning than do Japanese corporations which believe flexibility is more important. As a result, in most joint ventures in Japan, the American partner finds it necessary to assume the responsibility for the planning function relating to capital investment and new products leaving to its Japanese counterparts the day-to-day operating decisions. A series of surveys has been undertaken by Professor Kono of Hitotsubashi University on the subject of long-range planning. In his 1970 survey, 175 companies responded to his questionnaire out of 700 and, of these, 160 claimed to have long-range plans although the time span of the budgets for two-thirds of them was six months.[12] If it is assumed that most of those not responding to the questionnaire were not particularly interested in long-range planning, the results of the survey would indicate that there is less long-range planning on the part of private business in Japan than there is in the United States or Europe.

It can be assumed that most of the managers in the Japanese partner's organization will be well informed about management philosophies both Japanese and western. Approximately one thousand new books on management are published each year in Japan and some of these have become best sellers including a Japanese translation of Peter F. Drucker's Age of Discontinuity.[13] Of the new books on management published each year in Japan as many as nine percent are translations of foreign books. A Japanese translation of a book on goal setting by an American executive of Texas Instruments has also sold well in Japan.[14] In general, much of the management literature of Japan in the past has been inspired by foreign publications. On the occasion of the CIOS Management Congress in Japan in 1969, however several papers were presented by Japanese managers, many of whom have since joined other Japanese industrial leaders in writing about and developing Japanese management philosophies of international interest and application.

Regardless of the level of sophistication of the Japanese manager on matters relating to management practices and philosophy, staffing a wholly-owned subsidiary or joint venture in Japan is a problem particularly at the managerial level. Since management mobility is limited, the independent foreign company finds it necessary either to recruit college graduates or seek some of the limited number of Japanese managers who do not move from one firm to another. The young Japanese graduate attaches much significance to the name and reputation of the company with the result that, unless the foreign-owned company is well known such as IBM, NCR, Exxon (formerly Esso), RCA, Texas Instruments, or Caterpillar, it has difficulty in attracting the better graduates from the prestige Japanese universities. In joint ventures, if the Japanese partner has a good name and favorable reputation, it may be useful to rely upon the latter to secure the Japanese managers, some of whom may be supplied from the Japanese parent company and others recruited from among university graduates. Unfortunately, the Japanese partner under these conditions may consider the joint venture as a dependent entity owing its life and subsistence to the Japanese parent. If more discussion were devoted to personnel policies rather than capital contributions in reaching a joint venture agreement, a better understanding of the relationship would be accomplished at the negotiating stage, thereby avoiding difficulties and misunderstandings later on when the American partner may feel that the joint venture is not getting the best of the Japanese managerial talent.

In most managerial and personnel decisions, the Japanese company in a joint venture does in effect usually have more influence than the American partner. Such a situation evolves from the fact that:

1. frequently majority ownership is in the hands of the Japanese partner,
2. most of the employees including middle management are Japanese who are accustomed to working under Japanese management policies, and
3. the American partner, at the beginning particularly, finds it beneficial to let the Japanese company manage according to local conditions, leaning on the reputation of its Japanese partner in getting the new venture firmly established. Most important to the success of the firm is a spirit of cooperation and understanding between the parties to the venture rather than any particular American technique of organization and management.[15]

Most joint venture companies have two distinct groups of middle and upper managers: those recruited from the open market and those assigned by the Japanese partner. In order to avoid conflicts, such joint venture companies try to make sure that both groups receive comparable pay and status. Traditional Japanese employment practices are generally modified in joint venture companies to provide equal opportunities to competent managers regardless of age and college graduating class.

Another problem facing the foreign joint venture firm is that of finding Japanese managers who are bilingual. English, as taught in Japan, is primarily learning to read and write rather than to speak or understand the language. Although efforts to improve the teaching of conversational English are being made through special summer programs in the United States for Japanese instructors in English, far too few potential Japanese managers for joint venture firms have acquired a good working knowledge of conversational English even in college. When prospective Japanese employees speak good English it is usually due to their previous association with foreigners or foreign firms. If this is the situation, it is possible that the prospective candidate has not only left a Japanese firm but an American firm as well. Because of the customary low mobility of managers in Japan, the American manager would be well advised to explore the candidate's background rather thoroughly before making a decision to hire such a person.[16]

Just as the Japanese university education is general rather than professionally oriented, the kind of experience the Japanese manager gains in employment with a Japanese firm is quite different from that of an American in a U.S. company. The young graduate in the United States may start with one company, leave to join another company for broader experience, teach or do research for a while, and so forth, advancing in experience, authority, and responsibility as he moves from one employer to another. Unless the individual has been a drifter, this breadth of experience is considered an asset to his professional development. In Japan, such opportunities for breadth of experience with a number of employers is somewhat limited. With the exception of a few who enter graduate school for a teaching career, the top Japanese university graduates take positions with governmental ministries or with large Japanese companies with good reputations. Because of the lifetime employment system, those who seek work with an American company in mid-career are those, who, for some reason, have separated themselves from the traditional pattern either by choice or because the company for whom they were working has gone out of business. One outstanding Japanese manager in an American firm in Japan selected to go with a foreign company because illness upon his graduation from the university prevented him from being employed by a Japanese company at the same time as his classmates. Under Japanese traditional promotion practices, he would have remained behind his classmates once he took a job with a Japanese company. Others become dissatisfied with the slow pace of advancement in the Japanese firm and seek better opportunities in the foreign company.

When he goes with a foreign firm, the Japanese manager expects to find the traditional Japanese employment practices of identification with the company, "merit of years," lifetime employment, and eventual progress toward a high position upon retirement. American corporations in Japan are considered by the Japanese as large corporations from which is expected the same personnel policies as the large, reputable Japanese firms. When a young Japanese manager is hired for a fairly high level position, he expects to move up to the next higher position eventually. However, for most American firms in Japan, managers from the home office keep coming to take the top positions. Under such circumstances, the Japanese manager becomes discouraged as he begins to assume that he, as a matter of policy, is being excluded from a top management assignment.

In Japanese companies, the personnel department is generally much larger than that in American corporations and its director is usually responsible for all personnel activities and has coresponsibility with line managers. In the American company, on the other hand, the personnel manager may hold a staff position with functional authority to set procedures, policies, and standards with line managers, free to make decisions concerning personnel as long as such decisions do not conflict with company-wide policies and standards. The personnel departments in Japanese firms have the authority to move middle managers around throughout the company whenever such changes are beneficial to the employee's development. This practice is related to the traditional Japanese concept that individuals are not hired for specific jobs but are lifetime members of the company. Similarly, the training programs of the American corporations are primarily aimed at upgrading the employee's managerial and technical skills whereas those of the Japanese firm place more emphasis on the corporate image. However, young Japanese managers are beginning to prefer the American job-oriented policies with the result that labor mobility at the middle management level is increasing, thereby, making it easier for foreign firms and joint ventures to get competent people.

One of the reasons that job-oriented managerial positions appeal to the young Japanese is the fact that pay is related to the job rather than such circumstances as school, age, or length of service. On-the-job training practices of Japanese as opposed to foreign firms also reflect the difference between job-oriented and company-oriented personnel policies. In the Japanese company, the young manager is typically rotated from one job to another in a variety of functional areas such as sales, production, and personnel rather than in some functional area of specialization with movement through various divisions of the company. The Japanese middle manager following his company's job rotation training program, therefore, has little opportunity to become the kind of functional specialist which is being sought by the foreign firm.

Japanese managers recruited from the outside, therefore, have a variety of backgrounds depending upon the training they have had and the management philosophies of the companies from which they came. If several Japanese companies serve as the source of managerial personnel in the new venture, difficulties will be encountered in getting the group of work together. This problem may be particularly acute at the middle management level where under the Japanese ringisho system much cooperation is required at the lower levels in the decision-making and implementation process.

The larger Japanese companies, of course, initially recruit most of their managerial talent directly from schools and universities. The American subsidiary or joint venture will also want to select young potential managers from graduating classes and train them for responsible positions in the organization. Japanese university professors can be of great assistance in finding suitable candidates. RCA has been one United States corporation which recognized this fact and made contributions to a few key universities in the form of scholarship funds. IBM, on the other hand, has been successful in securing good candidates from graduating classes because of its employment practices and public relations efforts which eventually resulted in young Japanese considering IBM as a good place to work.

Some companies have done some recruiting of Japanese students at universities in the United States. Pfizer made a much publicized major recruiting effort for Japanese managers from American universities a few years ago.[17] Although Japanese educated in the United States have usually been carefully selected and, upon graduation, have a cross-cultural outlook, hiring such graduates may present some problems. If their education has been sponsored by a Japanese corporation, they have a responsibility to return to the organization which paid for their education and, if they do not do so, they will be looked down upon in Japan. Even those who have no obligations to a Japanese company may have difficulty in fitting into the American company's operation in Japan. His salary and status in the Japanese operation may be difficult to establish within the framework of the positions of the locally trained and educated Japanese managers who are of similar age and education within the company.

In a joint venture, personnel problems sometimes develop in the transfer of Japanese managers from the Japanese parent company to the joint venture. These transferees, like the American manager in the joint venture, are paid in accordance with the Japanese partner's policy including fringe benefits and expect to return to the Japanese parent after completing their assignments with the joint venture. Usually, these transferees are one of two types. One type are those who are assigned to work with the joint venture for the interests of the Japanese partner. Such an assignment is generally considered as training for a higher managerial post with the result that they are usually young, competent, and ambitious. Another type are the middle-aged department heads in the Japanese company who are nearing retirement because of their limited potential as prospective top managers. If this type of transferee begins to monopolize the higher managerial positions in the joint venture, it will be difficult to attract good managers from the outside.

The motive of the Japanese parent company in transferring or loaning managers to the joint venture will, therefore, have a significant effect on the extent to which this practice is or is not beneficial to the American venture. The transferred Japanese manager may be apprehensive about his assignment as he may feel that he is out of the mainstream with less chance of promotion than those remaining with the parent company. Under these conditions, his feeling of insecurity and dissatisfaction may affect the morale of others in the joint venture. At first, it may be necessary for the joint venture to rely upon staffing assistance from the Japanese parent company but as soon as possible, the joint venture should secure its own staff. Although assistance may be rendered by the Japanese company, the basic responsibility for hiring a permanent staff rests with the American party to the joint venture. If it is understood from the beginning that the joint venture is eventually to have its own managerial staff independent of the Japanese parent company, friction will be avoided and a loyal, harmoniously working group can be developed for the joint venture.[18]

The American top management in Japan is in a similar position to that of the transferee from the Japanese parent. Unfortunately the American manager sometimes spends much of his time and energies answering questions from the home office. Since he feels that this ultimate promotion depends more upon the opinions of the home office staff than on meeting the challenge of the Japanese operations, he may never truly get to understand the idiosyncrasies of his Japanese counterparts, a situation which is apt to result in misunderstandings and other difficulties.

Misunderstandings may result in differences of concepts concerning company goals, fairness, and saving face. In making decisions, the Japanese counterpart may be more concerned with harmony within the company and the market place as well as the company image, rather than a goal of profit maximization and dividends to stockholders. In fact, the Japanese do not have goals in the same sense as the American concept of this term. Japanese motivation is usually a result of activity rather than projected programs and objectives. Motivation is based on achieving what is good for the group or what will make the organization greater or healthier.[19]

Similarly, fairness in business as in other forms of association or intercourse in Japan is related also to the family-type image of those belonging to one's circle of association and those who do not. Once a person, a group of persons, or a corporation becomes a member (gift exchange relationship) of a given circle, the obligations incurred are matters of honor. As a result, American and Japanese concepts of fairness particularly as they relate to customers are different. In America, one thinks of the fairness of a decision with regard to all concerned. The Japanese manager on the other hand, considers fairness as it relates to a specific individual or company. To him not all customers are equal, some deserve and require more respect than others and he considers a decision as fair when it results in each person or company receiving the respect and consideration each is due. Therefore, for customers outside the circle, the Japanese concept of fairness carries with it only an estimate of possible gains or losses without the incurring of any continuing obligation. Business conducted, therefore, on the strict American style of making a sale or negotiating an agreement without an atmosphere of social cordiality and friendly exchange may result in a number of uncertainties which the Japanese may not consider fully binding.

Furthermore, the Japanese manager in the joint venture will also be reluctant to take a firm position on any matter until he is prepared to hold that position as a matter of honor. Whereas Americans tend to evaluate their actions and performance over the long run and the individual who, on the average, in his lifetime has been an honorable man is respected and admired in spite of ups and downs. The Japanese manager, on the other hand, finds life intolerable when faced with conflicting loyalties or obligations which he cannot resolve with honor. Consequently, he tries to avoid conflict with his American counterpart, so he will not be placed in a position when his honor may become at stake. In this connection, Japanese managers tend to take a group position in potential conflict situations particularly when they have been able to resolve their own differences before presenting a unified position to the American manager. Likewise, Japanese managers do not usually criticize each other's positions in front of top management.[20]

Because of these differences in basic concepts, it is more than the language barrier alone that makes it difficult for the American manager to communicate with his Japanese associates. The Japanese are particularly interested in getting to learn as much as they can about the foreign manager, hence, they ask many questions about his relationship with his wife, his children, his management, to see what kind of a man he is. To the Japanese he will always be an outsider and cannot become a true part of Japanese society except on the fringes through his participation in associations of which Japanese are also members. Communication can be achieved, however, if the American takes the time and patience to make a sincere effort to understand the Japanese. It is also true that only limited communication can result unless the Japanese manager makes an equal effort to learn about the culture and thinking of the American.

Another important technique for working effectively with Japanese managers is to avoid placing the responsibility for success or failure on any one individual. Under the traditional Japanese decision-making process, the final responsibility for group or company action rests with the president as the symbol of the company. Credit for success or blame for failure is therefore the company's not the individual. If the American top manager keeps this concept in mind he will avoid placing responsibility for success or failure on any one individual with the result that better relations will exist between himself and the Japanese managers.

Essential also to a smooth working relationship is the training and education of the Japanese managers in an understanding of the American way of doing things. As noted above, many postgraduate programs, seminars, and lectures are available in Tokyo and other major industrial centers for the training of Japanese managers in western techniques, policies, and decision-making. With an awareness of western business thinking, business practice, ethics, management concepts, and accounting standards, the Japanese manager in the American firm may be more likely to modify and adapt his own way of thinking to western philosophy and methods. Case studies and the use of quantitative methods provide common grounds for developing mutual understanding of both ways of thinking. Some Japanese managers in joint ventures have been brought to the United States for participation in training programs and for on-the-job experience in various divisions of the American parent company. This works well as being a booster for his morale on being chosen. Visits by executives of the American parent company to Japan and by the Japanese managers to the United States also help promote better communication and understanding. Japanese employees in American companies and joint ventures in Japan are usually very loyal to the company. Because of this loyalty success is achieved in spite of difficulties of communication.

Of major importance in the operation of any joint venture or subsidiary is the selection of the Americans who are sent to Japan to represent the American company's interest in the venture. It has been suggested that, insofar as possible, the American personnel should be assigned to staff or advisory rather than line positions.[21] Under these conditions, the American would be less involved in the ringisho decision-making process and, as an advisor or member of the staff he could communicate his thinking informally to those who would be in a position to influence the decision.

Regardless of the positions held by the Americans, they need to be mature and flexible in their thinking. They must understand also that underlying an outward appearance of western practices in Japan is an underlying culture which influences the reactions of the Japanese manager to the various situations which he faces. It is important, therefore, for the American manager to stop relying so much on a rational, logical, analytical approach to management and to study and observe the Japanese culture and its flexibility. Many Japanese consider themselves as a part of a superior culture and look down on Americans as not understanding the true harmony of life. The Japanese are extremely intelligent and quickly respond to ideas. American managers coming to Japan who have respect for their Japanese counterparts and who seek diligently to acquire an understanding of the Japanese culture will contribute much to the development of a successful subsidiary or joint venture in Japan.

Operating a business in Japan requires a fast pace of adaptation and decision-making. In most countries the economic growth rate is 2 to 4 percent per year in real terms whereas the Japanese economy is gaining at the rate of 12 to 14 percent. Japan is presenting a challenge to the world and a challenge to the American companies establishing affiliates whether wholly-owned or in the form of joint ventures.

In summary, therefore, the U.S. multinational corporation operating in Japan can secure and retain competent Japanese managerial talent as long as it understands traditional personnel practices and adapts its own policies to the Japanese culture. Training programs are available in Japan at the university and technical level to give the young Japanese manager an insight into western managerial philosophy and techniques. These need to be supplemented by on-the-job training in order to be effective. Short institutional and on-the-job training programs in the United States for the Japanese employee do much to enhance his effectiveness and add to his loyalty to the American corporation. Finally, the U.S. multinational corporation in Japan will be successful as long as its executives make a sincere effort to adapt its personnel, managerial, and decision-making policies and procedures to the Japanese way.

NOTES

1. See Robert J. Ballon, "Understanding the Japanese, Preparation for International Business," Business Horizons, vol. 13, no. 3 (June 1970): 28.
2. Robert J. Ballon, Doing Business in Japan, p. 32.
3. Maurice Bairy, "Motivational Forces in Japanese Life," The Japanese Employee, ed. Robert J. Ballon (Tokyo: Sophia University, 1969): 251-53.
4. Abegglen, James C. ed., Business Strategies for Japan, pp. 175-76.
5. Goyo Koyama, "Liberalization of Foreign Investment in Japan and Problems for Japanese Industries to Encounter," Management Japan, vol. 4, no. 4 (1971): 11.
6. See T. W. M. Teraoka, The Joint Venture in Japan—Accounting Aspects, Bulletin no. 32, (Tokyo: Sophia University, Socio-Economic Institute 1971): 45.

7. For detailed suggestion on negotiating with the Japanese partner see Francis T. Vaughan, Joint Venturing in Japan, Bulletin no. 30, (Tokyo: Sophia University Socio-Economic Institute, 1971).

8. Noritake Kobayshi, "Some Organizational Problems," in Joint Ventures and Japan, ed. Robert J. Ballon, pp 110-11.

9. Gen Numaguchi, "Komatsu Manufacturing Co. Ltd.—The Fusion of Japanese Managerial Philosophy and Modern Managerial Techniques," Management Japan, vol. 3, no. 3 (1969): 53.

10. "Texas Instruments—Sony Joint Venture," Management Japan, Special Issue (1968): 4.

11. See Shigeru Kobayashi, Creative Management.

12. Toyohiro Kono, "Long-range Business Planning in Japanese Enterprises," Management Japan, vol. 5, no. 2 (1971): 33-40.

13. Hideo Inohara, Importing Managerial Techniques, Bulletin no. 35, (Tokyo: Sophia University Socio-Economic Institute, 1972).

14. Charles L. Hughes, Goal Setting: Key to Individual and Organizational Effectiveness (New York: American Management Association, 1965).

15. Yotaro Kobayashi, "Human Aspects of Management," in Joint Ventures and Japan, ed. Robert J. Ballon, pp. 80-81.

16. Herbert Glazer, Development of Japanese Business Executives in Foreign Firms, Bulletin no. 13 (Tokyo: Sophia University Socio-Economic Institute, 1966): p. 8.

17. For a discussion of the general problem of staffing, see James C. Abegglen, ed., Business Strategies for Japan, Chapter Nine, "Recruiting for Operations in Japan," pp. 169-177.

18. Vaughn, op. cit.

19. Robert J. Ballon, Doing Business in Japan.

20. See Herbert Glazer, Development of Japanese Business Executives in Foreign Firms, Bulletin no. 13, (Tokyo: Sophia University Socio-Economic Institute, 1966).

21. Vaughn, op. cit., p. 16.

CHAPTER
6
**IMPLICATIONS FOR THE
LESS DEVELOPED COUNTRIES**

During the 1950s and 60s, the more highly developed and industrialized nations of the world, particularly the United States, offered a wide variety of financial and technical assistance as well as political and economic advice to the less developed nations. In many instances, the results of this assistance have been disappointing. Economic growth in the emerging nations has not measured up to expectations nor has it kept pace with population increases so that, for many countries, poverty and underemployment still prevail for the majority of the people.

Japan, on the other hand, has achieved a rapid economic development and an increase in standard of living for its people. The factors and conditions contributing to the growth of Japan should provide some insight into realistic approaches to enhancing the development of many emerging nations. Basically, Japan's growth has been attributable to industrialization rather than the exploitation of natural resources which it did not have. The primary causes of its rapid progress have been a hard working population, and government policies which have provided positive encouragement to continued growth and development.

CHARACTERISTICS OF DEVELOPMENT

A century ago, Japan was not much different from the less developed countries of today with an agriculturally-based economy characterized by "extreme poverty, undue pressure on land, traditional-bound technology and a peasant population held back by disease, malnutrition, and infanticide."[1] Without natural resources to serve as a source of capital, the Japanese government was successful in increasing substantially the productivity of its agricultural sector which it taxed heavily to help finance its initial industrial development programs and education. Some of the less developed countries might also consider concentrating on improvements in agricultural output as a means not only to provide a better living for their people but also to create surpluses which could be taxed to provide funds for improving education and stimulating industrialization.

Most of Japan's development during the last quarter of the nineteenth century can be attributable to its success in mobilizing the maximum efforts of its people and effective leadership which motivated the people to take action. In this connection, Japan did have some advantageous conditions which are not so prevalent in some of the less developed countries of today. Its centralized government, with loyalty to the emperor, was efficient and respected. Its people had a highly sophisticated cultural background and a strong sense of national unity.[2] Conflicts among the groups caused by differences in race, religion, tribal heritage, and the like, do not exist in Japan as they do in many of the developing nations. The rulers of Japan were anxious to make changes and they were receptive to western technology which was brought to the country by invitation rather than through colonial domination. This technology was therefore absorbed into the culture without damaging or partially destroying the cultural heritage of the people. As part of this heritage from the past, the characteristics of the Japanese people were conducive to development. These include curiosity, a readiness to try anything once, a receptiveness to new ideas, personal loyalties, and a strong sense of reciprocal obligation.[3]

Government provided leadership and encouragement in the adaptation of western technology and ideas for the development of the country. Following Japan's example, developing nations should give more attention to providing the kind of leadership which will stimulate their people to be diligent, industrious and dedicated to the task of working together. Development results from basic changes in ideas, attitudes, and institutions rather than from economic forces alone.

Those countries which have been successful in reaching a high degree of development vary widely in terms of their historical and geographic background. Yet they do have certain characteristics in common such as:
1. access to raw materials, natural resources, and power either through domestic production or importation,
2. a large amount of capital,
3. mass markets in terms of purchasing power and consumption stemming from a fairly large middle class with a somewhat equal distribution of income, and
4. advanced technology in terms of patents and know-how combined with skilled human resources, particularly qualified engineers and managers.

From the economic standpoint, therefore, the development of the emerging nations depends upon the extent to which such nations can acquire these characteristics.

With regard to natural resources, Japan has had to depend upon importation of essential raw materials and energy for its industrial development. Japan's rapid rate of expansion during the second half of the 1960s resulted in a doubling of its GNP from $100 billion in 1966 to $200 billion in 1970. During this same period, its exports also doubled from $10 billion to $20 billion. Energy and raw materials for this increase was acquired through importation. The consumption of petroleum in Japan increased from 92 million kilolitres in 1965 to 204 million kilolitres in 1970, of which 99.7 percent was imported. Similarly, with regard to raw materials, the consumption of iron ore was 46 million tons in 1965 and 111 million tons in 1970, of which 88 percent was imported.[4] Not having these natural resources itself, Japan has expanded its shipbuilding industry, its merchant fleet, and its international transportation system in such a way that many of its imported raw materials can be imported from sources thousands of miles away and delivered to the manufacturing or processing facility at a cost substantially below that which the U.S. manufacturer would have to pay for the same raw material produced in the United States and transported on American ships or land transporation to his plant in the United States. It is evident, therefore, from the Japanese experience that natural resources needed for development can be acquired either through importation or exploitation, provided the emerging nation recognizes the kind of needs it has and takes action to get the natural resources to processing and manufacturing units at a reasonable cost.

The transfer of capital is somewhat more difficult. In this connection, Japan attracted a substantial amount of private foreign capital during its early stages of industrial development between 1895 and 1913. In addition, the conservative consumption and saving habits of the Japanese helped create internal savings which served as a source of capital for further development. Government policies tended to stimulate private capital formation by taxation policies which permitted substantial inequalities in wealth and income. The Japanese government also encouraged the private sector to seek new opportunities to use this wealth in productive ways rather than in consumption or hoarding. As a further source of capital, Japan was able to build up its exports of silk, tea, and textiles at a time when these items were in great demand in the world market. Similar sources of capital are also available to the emerging nations today. In addition, large amounts of capital have been contributed by the developed nations either to international organizations and institutions or directly to the less developed nations to be used for economic and industrial development. From the standpoint of available capital, therefore, the developing nations of today are in a much better position to secure capital than Japan was during its early stages of development.

With regard to a mass market for its products, Japan was a large country from the standpoint of population at the time it began its industrialization. The size of its market was sufficient to permit an economical scale of production. Many developing countries, on the other hand, have a limited domestic market with the result that their producers of consumer goods manufacture in plants which are less than optimum size and whose costs are high. For countries with limited domestic demand, several countries have cooperated to form regional common markets in order to broaden the base for the sale of products and the sharing of resources. Even in a common market, economies of scale are difficult to achieve because each country tends to want to keep its small, high cost producers rather than become dependent upon another country's large-scale plant as a source of supply for any particular commodity. Governments, therefore, have a key role to play in encouraging low-cost production for growing domestic markets and in cooperating with other governments in helping create a sufficiently large market to take advantage of the economies of scale.

In this connection, Japan has learned that over-concentration on production to supply domestic and international markets has created problems of overcrowding in the cities, heavy strains on transportation, a shortage of land for industry, and problems of pollution of the environment. To overcome some of these disadvantages, Japan has started to import consumer goods to meet expanding demand rather than to increase productive capacity. For example, Japan's imports of textile goods from other Asian countries increased from $6 million in 1965 to $130 million in 1970. Its machinery imports from Asia also increased from $2.2 million in 1965 to $37 million in 1970.[5] Developing countries are also beginning to feel the adverse effects of concentrated industrial production in urban areas. In order to avoid some of the problems which Japan has encountered, the governments of these countries would be wise to take steps to encourage the regional diversification of their industrial production to the extent it is feasible and economical. In these countries, the development of an effective transportation and communications network within the country will be necessary to achieve a spreading of industry to small communities rather than a concentration in large metropolitan areas.

TRANSFER OF TECHNOLOGY

For the developed countries, goods, capital, and technology move more freely not only within the country itself but also among other advanced nations. With regard to technology, however, its transfer to the developing nation is much more difficult and complicated than its movement among developed nations. The transfer of technology from the developed to the less developed nations is one way and both countries have a responsibility to insure that the most appropriate technology is transferred. The less developed countries must establish goals and development plans to be used as criteria for the selection of the best technology to meet their social and economic objectives. The more advanced nations, on the other hand, need to work with the emerging nations in giving advice and economic cooperation in helping their economic development.

In order to acquire and adapt western technology to its economy, Japan not only brought engineers from the more advanced western countries but also sent its young engineers to study abroad and subsequently to return to work in industry and to train others to change traditional technology. To enhance the effectiveness of the adaptation of western technology to the Japanese economy, the Japanese government sent many missions overseas to learn and to seek the best technology for use in Japan. Machinery was imported and western engineers were hired to train Japanese engineers in the operation and maintenance of the equipment. Consequently, expansion of industry eventually took place through native Japanese technology with the result that 90 percent of the capital goods (machinery, equipment, etc.) recently have been supplied by Japan's domestic industry rather than being imported from abroad.

In addition to the practical training of engineers, Japan has also imported much technology through licensing agreements. During the past twenty years, as many as 10,000 licensing arrangements have been made with foreign corporations. In deciding which licensing agreements might be most beneficial for Japan, several companies might send specialists abroad to investigate new technology in their fields and to recommend which should be selected for Japanese use. In order to determine priorities for new technology, value judgments were made in economic terms based on the combined private and social benefits. In this connection, the policy adopted by Japanese government and industry was not to base new technological decisions primarily on the cheapness of labor or the cost of capital but on how the new technology might contribute to the long-term development and growth of Japanese society. Even greater flexibility in the choice of new technology and adherence to such a policy has become possible as Japan's international trade surplus has removed the constraints of a shortage of foreign currency.

In the initial stages of its development of assembly-type industries, Japan needed much foreign exchange for the importation of parts. As demand increased, the parts were manufactured in Japan and the raw materials imported. In these assembly-type industries as well as in other areas such as agriculture, public works, fishing, and textiles a choice can be made from varying degrees of technology ranging from extremely labor-intensive to capital-intensive. In other types of industries where certain types of machinery are required to manufacture the product, the range of choices between the use of capital as opposed to labor may be more limited. In processing industries such as chemical fertilizer, refining, petro-chemical, iron and steel, and cement, the relationship between labor and capital is fixed and, therefore, the transfer of the latest technology for the developed nations is most feasible.

The transferability of processing industries from the developed to the developing countries is very high and such transfers as usually beneficial to the developing nation provided certain characteristics prevail.[6] These characteristics include easy access to raw materials, a reliable and sufficient source of power, a good transportation system, qualified engineers, financing for the large capital investment required, and a large market growing at a sufficiently rapid rate to absorb the output of the plant.

Although the infrastructure may need to be expanded or improved to accommodate a process industry in a developing country, the physical transferability of such an industry is high. In the first place, a process industry is generally not dependent upon the existence of other industries; secondly, only a few qualified engineers need to be trained to operate the plant rather than a large number of skilled workers; and, thirdly, the technology is embodied in the plant with the result that it can be brought in under a turn-key contract and maintenance arrangement. The developing country benefits from the introduction of process industries as they encourage the establishment and expansion of the country infrastructure including power, transportation, ports, and education. Other types of industries both manufacturing and service can also take advantage of these improvements in infrastructure. Also new industries which use the products of the processing plant will be developed. In the planning and operation of a processing industry, techniques of market analysis, budgeting, network analysis, accounting, distribution, cost control, and the calculation of savings at the optimum level of production will be undertaken. Local managers and staff working with the foreign specialists will gain a practical knowledge of planning and control techniques of the type which are essential for a country's development.

THE ROLE OF SMALL-SCALE INDUSTRY

In the assembly and manufacturing industries, Japan has relied heavily on small-scale industry to maintain the kind of flexibility essential to orderly industrial development. Advanced technology has been selected for appropriate application in the large companies. For parts and accessories which did not require advanced technology for production, the larger companies have had subcontractual arrangements with small industries. The relationship between the small-scale company and the major company has been a close one, with the larger company frequently giving managerial, technical, and even financial assistance to its supplier.

Since the technology of the small-scale industry has tended to be labor-intensive, Japan has relied upon small business to provide employment for the majority of its people. These small companies also produce a wide variety of products to satisfy the needs of the country. Since, unlike the larger companies, they are not bound by a tradition of such personnel policies as lifetime employment, promotion and training from within, and various fringe benefits, the small companies are more flexible in adjusting to changes. As increased demand has justified the gradual introduction of more mass production technology in the larger companies, the small company suppliers have been able to absorb the impact as they do not require continued growth and expansion to provide advancement opportunities for their employees. Since small companies in Japan are not in competition with the larger companies but contribute to the economy in those areas where they are efficient, large-scale and small-scale industry are combined and integrated in such a way that each serves the needs of the other.

Both the larger companies and government-subsidized training institutions have encouraged small industry to increase efficiency through better management and production techniques. As communications and the transportation system continued to improve in Japan, many of these smaller companies developed in communities other than the main metropolitan and industrial areas. Likewise, as wages have increased and labor has become scarce in Japan, many of the larger companies are encouraging the development of small-scale suppliers in the less developed Asian nations for the manufacture of component parts and items requiring cheap labor.

Prior to World War II, the zaibatsu combines were virtually partners of the Japanese government and their leadership hastened the development of the country. The large family firms which made up this group in addition to new large companies have continued to play a role in the rapid postwar industrial growth of the country. The combination of large-scale and small-scale industry in Japan results in its economy being a mixture of extremes from the standpoint of industrial development. The big companies form a highly developed sector of the economy with heavy capital investment, large-scale operations, hired labor, and the application of the latest technology yielding a high per capita income. On the other extreme, is the pre-industrial or precapitalistic sector which is very small-scale at the artisan or family level with little capital and yielding a low income per capita. These small enterprises plus the small-scale industrial group account for a very high percentage of Japanese employment and contribute considerably to the total output of the country. Productivity and the wages of this group, however, are substantially below those of the larger, more highly industrialized firms.[7]

For the less developed countries, this role of small-scale industry in Japan may contain some characteristics appropriate for adaptation. Japan has always been deficient in natural resources and, in its early stages of development, lacked capital. At the same time, it had a large labor force seeking productive opportunities in industry. By encouraging entrepreneurship in small industries rather than replacing them with large-scale industries, Japan was able to provide employment opportunities and to absorb technology at a rate which served the best interests of the work force and industry by building into the economy the kind of flexibility needed for sound industrial development.

THE ROLE OF GOVERNMENT

In the economic and industrial growth of Japan, the government has been a positive factor working cooperatively with business and industry. It has provided the necessary social framework and improvements in infrastructure with which the people have been encouraged to develop the country's potential. In doing so, it has followed a policy of continuous action by not controlling directly the major part of the economy but by relying primarily on the freedom of the market forces for resource allocation. In order to stimulate sound economic growth, the government has acted as an innovator and entrepreneur, has given technical help to agriculture, has enforced stringent levels of taxation and has carried out the fundamental institutional reforms needed for development.[8]

In its pre-World War II development, Japan's policies were influenced by a fear of domination by foreign powers with the result that, along with economic development, governmental efforts were directed toward national political unity and an orderly society. This fear eventually resulted in an overemphasis on military industries rather than a balanced approach. However, the positive attitude of the Japanese government in creating a climate favorable to industrial development through the adaptation of western ideas did provide a sound base for the rapid growth of Japan following World War II.

The government played a positive role in the development of the country in a variety of ways. It eliminated the legal and political framework of the feudalistic system which had provided obstacles to the freedom of ownership, occupation, and movement. Governmental reforms in law, taxation, education and the like created an environment favorable to the emergence of new types of productive enterprises. Initially, government not only encouraged private enterprise but also stimulated development through actual entrepreneurship. Japan's policy, however, was not one of developing public enterprises in competition with the private sector but of using the vehicle of public ownership to establish new industries which were turned over to private enterprise as soon as they became sufficiently established to attract outside capital. In this connection, private capital formation was stimulated by permitting inequalities in wealth and income with the government's role being primarily that of encouraging new opportunities for the employment of this private wealth in productive enterprises rather than that of letting conditions develop which would lead to the consumption or hoarding of this wealth. In providing this encouragement, the Japanese government maintained a steady growth of credit and currency to supplement new financial mechanisms and institutions in creating and mobilizing purchasing power for its expanding economy.

By close cooperation with business and industry, the Japanese government was able to stimulate more development than a country like India where emphasis was on a mixed economy of private and public enterprise. In encouraging development, the Japanese government collaborated with big private business including:
1. the zaibatsu represented today by Mitsui, Mitsubishi, and Sumitomo,
2. the postwar groups which have formed around banks such as Dai-Ichi, Sanwa, and Nippon Kogyo, and
3. the large independent corporations exemplified by Toshiba (electrical goods), Yawata (steel), and Toyota (motors).

It would appear that the philosophy of the Japanese government has been to serve dominant interest groups such as big industry and, in turn, encourage such groups to serve the country. In pursuing such a philosophy, Japan basically has a capitalistic, free enterprise system. Because it worked through large corporations and combines, some felt that the Japanese government policies formed special interest groups at the expense of the welfare of the farmers, workers, and small entrepreneurs. However, economic growth with a resultant increase in the standard of living of all seems to be particularly slow in those countries which have used a socialistic approach in an effort to reach a compromise over the issues of various class interests and has taken place most rapidly in countries operating under a predominantly private enterprise system.

In the agricultural sector, Japan also emphasized development by introducing land reforms which were designed in such a way to increase agricultural production rather than merely to divide the land up among the people with little consideration of the effect on output. Too frequently developing nations have been pressured to undertake land reform for social rather than economic reasons as a condition for international economic aid. In such instances, agriculturally productive land which has been divided up among tenant farmers tends to lose much of its efficiency resulting in a reduction in output and a disruption of the less developed country's agricultural base. Many reforms and changes which are based upon political and social objectives tend to have a retarding effect on development unless equal attention is given to the economic aspects of the changes.

EDUCATION

In improving the standard of living of its population, governments must provide the necessary social framework within which people are encouraged to develop the country's resources. In the case of Japan, the government's attitude toward education was particularly beneficial for development. The educational system was expanded and modernized in response to economic needs. Japan exploited fully the use of foreign skills and training to strengthen its educational institutions. Classical learning was replaced by emphasis on western science and industrial techniques. Combined with this was strong governmental support of a national system of education.

In modernizing its educational system in 1872, Japan studied the systems of the United States and the advanced European countries. Initial emphasis was on a broad system of elementary schools open to all children regardless of sex and social backgrounds. By 1945, the enrollment ratio for the first six years of compulsory education was 99 percent and 70 percent of the graduates of the elementary schools went on to programs of the lower secondary schools.[9] Beyond the elementary level, the Japanese government recognized the importance of industrial education for the training of middle-class technicians at the secondary level and the development of higher education in technology and engineering. Under the command of the Allied Occupation Forces immediately after World War II, Japan reformed its educational system and extended compulsory education through the lower secondary school under a new 6-3-3 plan. (For a summary of the Organization of the School System of Japan see Chart. 5.)

CHART 5

ORGANIZATION OF THE SCHOOL SYSTEM

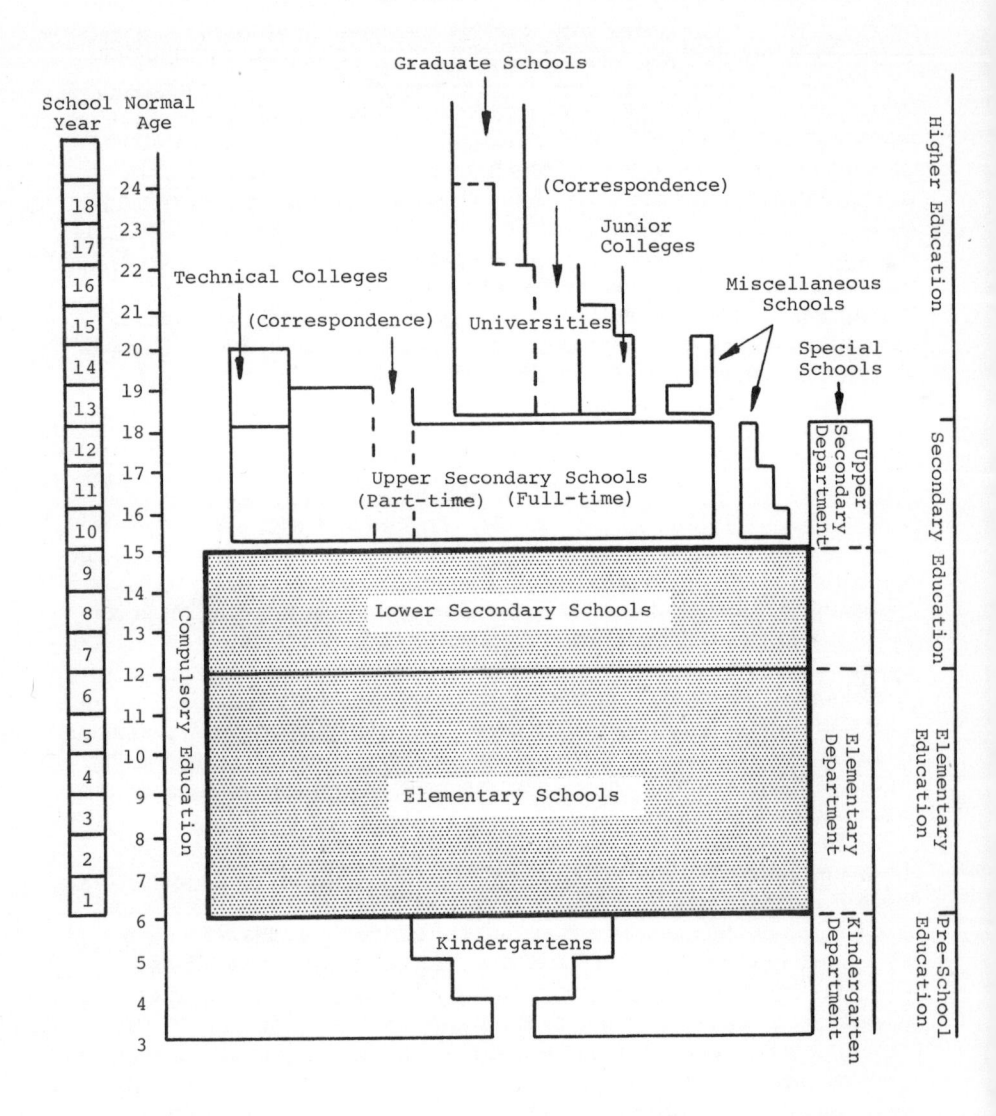

Source: Japanese National Commission for UNESCO, Japan--Its Land, People and Culture, 3d ed.,(Tokyo:University of Tokyo Press, 1973), p. 201.

The occupation forces also insisted on the establishment of new four-year liberal arts colleges with the first two years devoted to general rather than specialized education.

The establishment of these new institutions marked the beginning of an explosive expansion of higher education in Japan. Since the establishment of Tokyo Imperial University in 1886, only two other national universities had been created by 1918: Kyoto and Tokoku. As part of these national universities, an institute of technology and an institute of agriculture were also established. A number of private colleges and universities were formed during this period but they were not officially accredited by the Japanese government. It was these private universities which undertook innovative and practical approaches to higher education by readily adapting to the needs of a changing society.

Between 1918 and 1945, these private institutions, such as Waseda, Keio, Meiji, Hosei, Chuo, Nihon, Kokugakuin, Doshisha, and others, were given formal university status by the government. It was during this period that the university system of Japan was expanded and emphasis placed on professional training. By 1945, Japan had a diversified system of higher education including 48 universities with an enrollment of about 100,000 students, plus about 300 colleges and 100 teacher training institutions. By 1969, there were 852 universities with more than 1,600,000 students representing about 20 percent of the appropriate age group.[10] Along with the rapid expansion has been an increased emphasis on general education and less on professional skills, with a consequent lessening of the relevance of higher education to the needs of industry and business.

The private colleges and universities have taken the lead in developing programs for the training of personnel for business and industry during this postwar period. These include the graduate degree programs of Keio University and Sophia University, the undergraduate programs of the Institute of Business Administration and Management, and the various courses offered by management associations. In 1972, Tejin Ltd., one of the largest synthetic fiber manufacturers in Japan, constructed a complex of advanced training facilities at the port of Mt. Fuji. Upon completion, these were turned over to a newly organized corporation, Fuji Insititute of Education and Training which makes these facilities available to various organizations and institutions for training purposes. Semigovernment supported institutions organized since World War II include the Academy of Management Development of the Japan Productivity Center (1965) and the Institute for International Studies and Training (1969) which operates under the general supervision of the Japanese Ministry of International Trade and Industry.

The experience of Japan in creating and maintaining an educational system has significance for the less developed countries. Compulsory elementary education to build a literate population is a basic requirement for any kind of development whether agricultural or industrial. The transfer of knowledge and skills can only take place effectively among people who are literate. Even the simplest occupations in modern society require some ability to read and write.

At the secondary level of education, training in technical and vocational skills is particularly important for the majority of the young people in a developing country. The continuation of academic instruction and apprenticeship training of the type existing in Germany is a particularly useful approach to provide practical skills. Initially, business and industry are not well equipped in an emerging nation to cooperate in this kind of educational partnership without the assistance and encouragement of the government.

At the level of higher education, it was found in Japan that innovative and modernizing approaches came through the efforts of the private institutions. As the programs of these educational establishments were found to be of the type contributing to the development of the country, the Japanese government gave them academic accreditation and, in some instances, financial assistance. In the developing nations, governments need to be alert to the contributions being made by the private colleges and universities and to be flexible in granting recognition to those institutions which are providing educational programs related to the developing needs of the country. All too frequently, state educational institutions become politically entrenched and resist change with the result that they influence their governments to maintain a status quo in higher education. Japan's eventual recognition of the innovative private universities was a stimulating force in the country's development.

DISTRIBUTION AND TRANSPORTATION

In addition to building an appropriate educational system, Japan also developed a distribution and transportation structure designed to fit its economy. Since Japan has few natural resources, it has to depend upon remote overseas sources for most of its oil, coal, iron ore, non-ferrous metals, and timber. Japan's dependence upon imports of basic national resources is illustrated in Table 1. In terms of quantity, Japan imports 350 million tons a year against exports of 40 million tons.[11] As a result, its industries, particularly those requiring large quantities of heavy raw materials such as the iron and steel industry, are located near seaports. Similarly, its industrial power is generated close to the coastline where fuel is imported. To insure

TABLE 1

Japan's Dependence on Overseas Nations for Its
Raw Materials, 1968
(unit: 1000 tons)

Item	Total Demand	Overseas Dependence Rate
iron ore	77,437	84.7%
cooking coal	43,650	71.9
copper	197	73.4
lead	81	56.5
zinc	290	53.8
aluminum	657	100.0
nickel	60	100.0
petroleum	799,000 kl	99.5
lumber	91,806,000 M^3	46.7

Source: Report of the Resources Study Committee of the Economic Council.

a supply of basic resources, the Japanese government stimulated the construction of modern port facilities and the development of a strong shipbuilding industry and a shipping fleet.

For domestic transport, Japan created an efficient rail system supplemented by super highways in the more populated areas. As Japan places increased emphasis on the regional diversification of consumer goods industries, greater strains will be placed upon the internal transportation system. Plans are underway to build additional parallel railroad tracks and more high speed trains to meet the demand for rapid transit.

Positive government policies in the initial development of a railway system and good port facilities contributed much to the economic growth of Japan. Too frequently, the less developed nations have neglected their railroads, have failed to construct efficient highways, and have been slow in modernizing their port facilities. Equally important as the facilities themselves, are the ease of movement of goods and the security related to their transportation and storage. Effective maintenance and scheduling of rolling stock are also essential elements of a good transportation network. For their economic development, emerging nations can learn from Japan the necessity of an efficient transportation and distribution system tailored to meet the country's particular needs.

With regard to distribution, the large private general trading companies of Japan have played an important role in marketing innovations. Although there are many specialized trading companies in other countries, the general trading company is peculiar to Japan. Initially, these companies acted as wholesale merchants but eventually expanded into related activities such as market research, financing, buying and selling products both domestically and overseas, commodity markets, foreign exchange, transportation, insurance, and storage services. At one time prior to World War II, Mitsui and Company, a large, financially strong general trading company controlled some of the main parts of the Japanese economy from natural resources to finished products with sales exceeding the national budget of Japan.[12] After the War, the Allied Occupation Forces broke up the zaibatsu companies such as Mitsui and Mitsubishi into hundreds of smaller companies. Because of the rapid economic growth of Japan since the War, many of these smaller, newly created companies, grew large through the application of technical and distributive innovations. By grouping, diversifying, and simplifying distribution channels, these companies caused extensive changes in the traditional methods of distribution resulting in better communications, coordination, and administration.

In order to take maximum advantage of their position as general traders, some of the larger companies have created distribution channels which include production, processing, transportation, insurance, storage, financing and retailing. By linking producers more closely with consumers through rearranging and reorganizing existing groups of wholesalers and agents, the general trading companies have been able to lower distribution costs. Such companies have also become directly linked with supermarkets, department stores, manufacturers, farmers and the like, resulting in merchandise being made available to consumers at lower prices. A few shopping centers have been financed and constructed by these trading companies. Large warehouses and distribution centers have also been set up for local as well as overseas marketing of raw materials, semifinished products and consumer goods including food. Unlike conglomerates which have been created through merger in the United States, the general trading company of Japan has grown by expanding its functions to include many aspects of efficient distribution.

In the developing nations, much more emphasis needs to be placed on innovative approaches to distribution. A 15 percent reduction in the cost of distributing passed on to the consumer would result in a 15 percent increase in the standard of living of the population. In Japan, innovation has come through private enterprise in the form of the general trading companies. Although such companies may become extremely large and control highly integrated segments of the economy, efforts on the part of the governments of developing nations to set up distribution channels either through direct financing or the encouragement of cooperatives have not resulted in substantial increases in efficiency or in a reduction of the cost of distribution. One possible solution for the developing nations might be the encouragement of large retail marketing chains to reduce costs and to provide the kind of buying power which would assist in creating more efficient farming, manufacturing, and transportation operations. To make such improvements in distribution effective, governments have a responsibility to strengthen transportation and communication systems and to ease the flow of goods by eliminating red tape and insuring that transportation channels do not become a source of petty graft by those who administer and control them.

GROWTH OF PRIVATE INDUSTRY

Concentration on the development of strong sales and distribution networks as opposed to production alone has been a characteristic of private Japanese corporations which have grown most rapidly in the postwar period.[13] Other characteristics of these high growth companies have been the development of new products and creativity in product and technical research. As a means of becoming more creative, top management in Japanese companies has tended to rely more heavily on a group decision-making approach in introducing new products and expanding facilities. Strategic planning departments and research and development have also been characteristics of those Japanese companies which have grown rapidly. Such companies also use task forces and managers of special projects to introduce change. Innovation in these companies has also frequently resulted in changes in the organizational structure as well as changes in traditional rules and regulations. Those companies which have been successful in maintaining flexibility in the organizational structure have tended to achieve a higher growth rate particularly since 1960.

With regard to top management in those more rapidly growing Japanese companies, there seems to be little or no relationship between the age and educational background of the members of the top management and the rate of growth of the company. On the other hand, differences in the decision-making process among the various companies have been found to have a relationship to growth. The four main characteristics of the decision-making process of high-growth companies in Japan have been:
1. flexibility in gathering information and forecasting,
2. willingness to undertake risky innovations,

3. listening to the opinions and ideas of subordinates in developing and evaluating ideas, and
4. proper timing.

The managers of high-growth companies recognize that conditions are constantly changing and are willing to maintain an open mind and to make decisions based upon the current situation without being prejudiced by solutions and experiences of the past. As a result, successful expanding companies engage in long-range planning as a means of developing strategies for the future and of enabling management to see situations with a flexible mind.

Similarly with regard to innovations, the top managers of the rapidly expanding companies are interested in new ventures, products, and markets and forecast the risks involved taking the latter into account in choosing among alternatives. In low-growth companies, the managers are satisfied with gradual improvement within the framework of what they are already doing since they tend to fear the risk of failure in a new venture.

Although the top managers of high-growth companies are generally full of ideas, they also rely upon their staffs and planning departments to supplement these ideas, and to gather additional information as a means of determining a course of action. Such managers also maintain an open mind and welcome ideas from outside the company. On the other hand, the top managers of low-growth companies tend to be indifferent to many of the ideas of their staff personnel and seem to be more interested in administering the enterprise and in controlling its personnel than thinking up new ventures. Although the majority of such managers seem to be interested in ideas coming up from below in the organization, they reach decisions late and are generally much slower in taking action than the managers of the high-growth companies.

In this connection, proper timing is extremely important. High-growth companies such as SONY keep one step ahead of competitors in taking the risk in product innovation and technological advance. Such companies, however, do weigh carefully the risks involved and take them into account in making the decision.

Decision-making, planning, innovation and the like, by themselves, do not result in industrial growth. Behind each successful company is a decision-making leader who has guided the organization to prosperity through his creativity, knowledge, rich experience, systematic thinking and ability to lead and motivate those who work for him. The critical component of the growth of Japanese private industry, therefore, has been a group of top executives and leaders who have taken the initiative in aggressive expansion of business. Yet their leadership and managerial capabilities would not have been effective without highly reliable supporting systems of qualified, literate employees, able managers, and top-flight executives in key positions.

Although most of the developing countries tend to have weak supporting systems in this respect, they do have excellent industrial leaders in many kinds of business activity. In order to achieve growth, positive governmental policies are needed to encourage creativity innovation, company groupings, flexibility, and constructive decision-making by these leaders. Private industrial growth has been the key to Japanese development and it has only been possible because the government itself has maintained flexible plans which have been related to the changing needs of the economy and which permit innovation in development. Too often the governments of emerging nations adopt a policy of government ownership and control of basic industries, thus limiting the industries in which private enterprise is permitted to function. Under such a mixed economy, the top management of the government corporations tend to be either politically oriented or bureaucratic and make decisions in a manner similar to the managers of the low-growth industries in Japan. Since the integrated and innovative growth potential of the private sector industries is limited under such an arrangement and since private industry is frequently dependent upon state-owned enterprises for its raw materials and certain supplies, much of its leadership and decision-making freedom is stifled, resulting in a rate of growth which is scarcely sufficient to offset population increases. Developing countries which have achieved a fairly high degree of independence from international economic aid have had the kind of governments which have created a climate for private initiative and innovative, progressive management.

THE AUTOMOTIVE INDUSTRY IN DEVELOPING COUNTRIES

Illustrative of a rapidly growing part of private enterprise in Japan has been the automotive industry. In 1955, Japan produced approximately one half of one percent of the total number of cars and trucks manufactured in the United States, West Germany, the United Kingdom, France, Italy, and Japan. By 1969, Japan's share of the total automotive production of these countries was 18 percent.[14] The nature of the growth of Japan's automotive industry may have some significance in terms of policies appropriate for the automotive industry in developing nations.

Up until 1955, the production of three-wheeled trucks in Japan exceeded that of the four-wheel variety. The manufacture of three-wheelers reached a peak in 1960 and they have now been replaced by four-wheeled trucks. Trucks have accounted for a large portion of

Japanese automotive production and it was not until 1969 that the production of passenger cars exceeded that of four-wheeled trucks. Most passenger cars and trucks produced in Japan have been small sized. Until 1968 most of the passenger cars were used by business, by government, and as taxis, and the small trucks by medium and small-scale enterprises. Since then, the rapid rise in national income has resulted in an increased demand for passenger cars for personal use in Japan, with the result that the majority of the production of the Japanese automotive industry in the 1970s has been passenger vehicles rather than trucks and buses. In the export market, sales of Japanese passenger cars exceeded those of trucks as early as 1965, and by 1970 Japan was one of the world's largest automobile exporters.

One of the reasons for the success of Japan's development of automotive export markets was the modernization of its production facilities to meet international standards during the early part of the 1960s. For example, Toyota's Kamigo Factory for the manufacture of engines and transmissions was completed in 1965 and was equipped with fully automatic machines and materials handling devices. These automated machines were built in Japan to Toyota's specifications. The company's assembly plant in Takaoka is a mass production facility controlled by computer and has an annual capacity of more than 600,000 vehicles, making it one of the largest automobile assembly plants in the world. Nissan also has a large assembly plant with a 500,000 annual capacity. Many of the automotive parts factories in Japan have also been modernized and automated. Consequently, Japan's competitive position in the world's automotive markets is not attributable to low wage costs but to modern, automated factories maintaining high quality standards. By 1966, Japan's labor productivity level in its automotive industry exceeded that of Western Europe and by 1969, rose to 9 cars per year per employee compared to 14-15 per year per employee for the United States.

Japan's automotive industry was stimulated through the government's policy of road construction in the 1950s. The development of effective road transportation also led to more regionally diversified development and industrialization. Since the modernization and utilization of roads and transportation is necessary for industrial and agricultural expansion, many developing countries, in addition to improving roads, are making efforts to establish their own automotive industries. However, this industry requires a sophisticated technical and engineering know-how in a variety of different fields. In fact, the average compact car is made up of 60 different raw materials, has an average of 2,500 major parts and assemblies made up of about 20,000 items. The production of an automobile, therefore, requires some knowledge of the manufacturing processes and the functional characteristics of the several thousand elements that make up the total assembly.

For developing countries planning the establishment of their own automotive industries, Eiji Toyoda, President of the Toyota Motor Company, Ltd. has suggested that certain conditions be fulfilled and that the industry be developed gradually.[15] The plan for the development of the automotive sector should be based upon the level of sophistication of industry as a whole within the country. The markets and manufacturing facilities should be planned in terms of a region with a sufficient potential demand to take advantage of some of the economics of scale which perhaps can only be achieved through common market agreements with neighboring countries. In order to insure the proper development of the industry, the cooperation of international automotive firms from the developed nations is needed. Such international companies can assist in providing technology, in training workers, in developing parts manufacturers, and in setting up assembly plants.

Similar to Japan, it would seem most appropriate for the automotive industry in a developing nation to start with trucks and buses as these are essential for the economic development of the country because they increase the mobility of the work force and provide improved transportation of goods and materials.

The steps suggested for the setting up of an automotive industry in a developing country might be the following:
1. develop service facilities and train mechanics,
2. educate the people on good driving practice and vehicle care,
3. establish manufacturing or rebuilding facilities for those replacement parts which are frequently needed and which do not require a high level of technology and skill to produce,
4. set up assembly plants and tie them in with the plants producing replacement parts,
5. begin the manufacture of more complex components such as axles, engines, gear boxes, and suspension units,
6. expand manufacturing to include an integrated automatic manufacturing industry.

These suggestions for the development of an automatic industry represent a practical approach to industrial growth. Too frequently emerging nations attempt to undertake the full scale development of an industry before the economy or the people are sufficiently advanced to use the products effectively. Under such circumstances, political or nationalistic considerations tend to overshadow the economic aspects in the decision-making process. The attitude of developing countries toward cooperation with and encouragement of multinational companies such as those in the automotive industry also has an effect on the extent to which an industry can be developed in accordance with these suggestions.

THE ROLE OF INTERNATIONAL ESTABLISHMENTS

Predicated upon the principles of free trade, multinational corporations have grown rapidly since World War II. Although the establishment, acquisition, and merger of business enterprises are legitimate activities in a free economy, the behavior of the multinational companies has not always conformed to the so-called national interest of some of the countries where they have located. Japan's Ministry of International Trade and Industry has suggested the formulation of international criteria to govern the behavior of multinational corporations as a prerequisite to completing the liberalization of the country's foreign capital investment policies. In some respects, therefore, Japan shares some of the anxieties of the less developed countries concerning the role of the multinational corporation in the economy. Since Japan achieved much of its development prior to the rise of the multinational corporations, one cannot use the Japanese experience as a basis for evaluating the contribution of such companies to developing nations. Yet, because of the benefits which the multinationals have brought to the emerging nations in which they have located, it seems appropriate to consider them as one of the forces for economic growth in the less developed countries.

In addition to the financial investment made by these multinational corporations, they also bring technology, employment, training programs for managers and workers, and the like. Although developing countries frequently complain of the profits which such companies make, they tend to overlook the fact that such profits are small when compared to the benefits to the national economy. Since many of these multinational companies have total sales in excess of the GNP of some of the countries in which their branches are located, some governments fear their size and feel that the company's interests are worldwide with decisions being made by foreigners who are not concerned with the problems of the emerging country. From the standpoint of the multinational corporation, it is frequently felt that the governments of the developing nations meddle too much in the company's private affairs. Yet, modern corporations recognize that their welfare is based upon cooperating with the country in achieving the latter's aspirations.

In commenting on the relationship between developing countries and the multinational corporation Luitzen E. Jan Brouwer, Senior Managing Director of the Royal Dutch/Shell Group of Companies stated as follows:

> You may tell me that I am naive to emphasize only the rational aspects of foreign investments; to talk only about long-term economic cost and benefits; to point triumphantly to the impact on employment, to growth, to its

contribution to new technology, to its effect on the balance of payments, and so on. Naive, because the receiving government has sometimes more immediate problems. Such lofty detachment as I advocate is not easy in the confusion of local short-term politics. And it may become almost irrelevant under those conditions to point out that executives of multi-national corporations are not concerned with power but only with the wellbeing of their corporations, which is usually inextricably mixed with the long term economic wellbeing of the countries in which they operate. Yet, this is in general the case. Their concern not only embraces profitability but all the things mentioned before and, importantly, also being a good employer and—perhaps most surprising of all—being a good corporate citizen. As the Chairman of Unilever has put it: "In any country where we persistently disregarded the public interest we should be unlikely to have a business for long."[16]

Responsible multinational companies identify themselves with the economics of the nations where they are located and attempt to set long-range goals and policies which are compatible with those of the host country. Yet, in doing so, such companies recognize that their major function is to operate efficiently and profitably at a level which will insure their continued existence in the world of competition. The governments of developing nations in attracting foreign investment must recognize this and give fair and equitable treatment to the foreign corporation and its property by protecting the company from short-term political pressures. Without this kind of stability and dependability on the part of the government of the developing country, additional foreign investment will be discouraged. Restrictions which prevent the most effective mobilization of capital, technology, managerial skills, equipment, and people may, in the long run, harm the national interest and make it difficult for the multinational corporations to make a maximum contribution to the economy.

With regard to financing, international lending agencies have also played a role in strengthening the economies of the developing nations by providing funds and technical assistance for the construction of industrial plants. Loans from the World Bank, the Asian Development Bank, the Interamerican Development Bank, and other international monetary institutions are usually preceded by a feasibility study and supplemented by consulting assistance. The United Nations through its development program also recommends international consultants and maintains its own staff of specialists to help developing nations determine the best projects to undertake. As part of its economic assistance program, countries such as the United States and Japan also offer consulting services for those projects which they consider appropriate for the developing nations.

With regard to aid to the developing nations, the Japanese government has committed itself to increasing its foreign aid to one percent of its GNP which means an annual contribution of $3 billion in the near future. In addition, Japan has agreed to increase its aid to private industry through the Export-Import Bank. In administering its aid program, Japan may use some of its consultants who have been concerned with finding new projects in their areas of specialization for adoption by foreign governments and international institutions.

In summary, therefore, Japan's development is relevant to the problems of economic growth in the emerging nations. Basic to Japan's success has been a positive government policy of building infrastructures, of strengthening education, of cooperating with the private sector, of helping with financing, stimulating growth through relatively free market forces, and of creating a climate for development by maintaining a high degree of political stability. In the private sector, development has been stimulated by innovative leadership, flexible organizational structure and policies, in-plant training, associations of top managers, assistance to small-scale industry, importation of the most appropriate technology, a national loyalty, and, more recently, overseas expansion. Essential also to the development of Japan has been the positive attitude of the people themselves toward hard work and education. The increase in per capita income in Japan has been further accentuated through low population growth rate more similar to that of western society than the high rate of the less developed nations.

Japan's rapid development has also resulted in problems similar to those of other highly industrialized nations. Heavy concentration of industry, increased urbanization, crowded highways, and lack of living space have created problems of ecology which are threatening to darken the land of the rising sun. These and other elements of change are causing Japanese management to think in terms of new technologies and revised policies and practices to meet the challenges of Japan's future development more effectively.

NOTES

1. Ali, Zaman, and Baset, Economic Development of Japan (Dacca: Ideal Library, 1967), p. 137.
2. Angus Maddison, Economic Growth in Japan and the USSR (New York: W. W. Norton, 1969), p. 78.
3. Ali, Zaman, and Baset, op. cit., p. 130.

4. S. Okita, and S. Tamura, Monograph on "International Cooperation through the Transfer of Processing Industries," presented at the VIII Conferencia Interamericana de Gerencia, Caracas, September, 1973, p. 2.

5. Ibid.

6. For a detailed study of this topic see Shuji Tamura, "Economics of Scale and Technological Progress of the Japanese Petrochemical Industry and Their Implications for Development Planning," (Ph.D. dissertation, Stanford University, 1971).

7. Seymour A. Broadbridge, Industrial Dualism in Japan, pp. 5-7.

8. Angus Maddison, op. cit., p. 79.

9. Japanese National Commission for UNESCO, Japan, Its Land, People, and Culture, p. 200.

10. Nagai Michio, Higher Education in Japan, Its Take-Off and Crash (Tokyo: University of Tokyo Press, 1971), p. 45.

11. Hayashi Shuji, "The Roles of Distribution and Transportation in the Growth of the Japanese Economy", Management Japan, vol. 4, no. 1 (1970): 13.

12. Yoshizo Ikeda, "Distribution Innovation in Japan and the Role Played by General Trading Companies," Management Japan vol. 4, no. 2, (1970): 19.

13. Much of the following concerning high growth companies was excerpted from Torohira Kono, "An Analysis of Corporate Growth in Japan," Management Japan, vol. 3, no. 4 (1970): 30-36.

14. Information concerning the development of Japan's automotive industry was taken from an article entitled, "Analysis of the Structure of Japan's Automobile Industry from the International Viewpoint" by Professor Yoshiro Miwa of Senshu University in Management Japan, vol. 4, no. 2 (1970): 22-28.

15. Eiji Toyoda "Developing Countries and the Automotive Industry," Management Japan, vol. 5, no. 3 (1971): 6.

16. Luitzen E. Jan Brouwer, "Mobility of Capital and Resources," Management Japan, vol. 3, no. 3 (1969): 10.

CHAPTER

7

JAPANESE MANAGEMENT IN THE 1970s

Rapid industrialization and economic expansion have created problems for Japanese management. Industrial pollution has caused an increased emphasis on the social responsibility of business enterprises. The worldwide expansion of Japanese investment and distribution has created the need for changes in the organization of enterprises and an increased awareness of the importance of relations with other nations. Research and development, personnel administration and even the decision-making process itself are being reconsidered by Japanese managers in light of changing conditions. With the rapid expansion of the worldwide activities of Japanese firms, the international outlook of both government and business has been changing.

ENVIRONMENTAL PROBLEMS

Environmental problems have become the concern of industrialized countries throughout the world. In Japan, the Basic Law for Pollution Countermeasures was passed in August 1967, but it was not until 1971 that an Environmental Protection Agency was established and a committee of experts formed within Japan's Economic Council to undertake research on environmental pollution.[1] During 1971, three court cases were decided in Japan under which the corporations were found guilty of unlawful acts of disease-type pollution of the environment and were ordered to pay large sums in compensation. The investment of Japanese companies in pollution control devices has increased rapidly in Japan. Although the investment in production facilities increased 3.3 times from 1965 to 1970, the investment in pollution control devices increased 5.5 times during the same period. Whereas the share of investment in pollution control was only about 3 percent until 1968, it was 5 percent in 1969, 5.3 in 1970, 9.1 in 1971, and as high as 11.5 in 1972.[2]

Prime Minister Kakuei Tanaka in his "A Proposal to Remodel the Japanese Archipelago,"[3] written prior to his election, recommended programs of industrial relocation, controlled urban growth and other plans to keep Japan's environment from deteriorating. Although Japanese managers might not agree with Prime Minister Tanaka's concepts and programs, they would agree that they had been primarily concerned with expansion and industrialization without paying much attention to the problems of environment or to the conservation of natural resources. As in most developed countries, the environment was considered outside the control of private enterprise. However, in the 1970s Japanese companies have come to recognize their social responsibility for environmental protection and many have established anti-pollution committees or similar departments reporting to top management.

As a result, the selection of new technology and plant sites has included an analysis of the effect on the environment in addition to the economic factors alone. One solution to the problem has been to consider the locating of environmental-consuming plants in the developing nations where the effect of pollution of the environment would not be so severely felt as in Japan. Most recognize, however, that this is not a substitute for a scientific approach to improving technology to reduce pollution but a means of mitigating the adverse effect of increased industrialization within Japan itself. In general, progressive Japanese management has come to recognize the need to shift emphasis from expansion alone to qualitative growth which promotes the welfare of the people.

MANAGEMENT CONCEPTS

As Japanese management broadens its thinking to include the welfare of society, its functions tend to broaden. Similar, among the younger generation, a new sense of values is developing in Japan as well as in other developed nations whereby flexibility in organizational structures and objectives become necessary. Organizational units are being restructured in terms of objectives, problems, and anticipated results. Computer-based management information systems have resulted in less departmental thinking and a more thorough review of the organization's operational efficiency. In the traditional Japanese organization, teamwork and a seniority-based sense of order cemented the people to the enterprise and gave them a feeling of security. The organizational reform underway in Japan is creating some apprehension in that the new work environment may not provide as much security as the traditional Japanese management system of lifetime employment, teamwork operations, and the "ringi" system of decision-making. As a result of this changing managerial approach, greater stress is being placed on the promotion of individuals on the basis of performance and ability rather than seniority, the development of specialists and strategic planning.

The gradual change in emphasis from a seniority based management structure to an ability-oriented management can be attributed to a number of conditions emerging during the latter part of the decade of the 1960s and the beginning of the 70s. Changes in the Japanese economy included:
1. a need to create markets for products,
2. a shift from a labor surplus situation to one of a labor shortage, and
3. a liberalization of the movement of trade and capital.

With regard to the types of jobs and workers, there was a shift from mechanical to equipment-centered industry requiring highly skilled technicians, and many more high school graduates not all of whom had the ability to assume industrial positions. The younger generation attached more value to functional skills than organizational association. The workers, themselves, began to demand better human relations and more independence to offset the bureaucracy of large enterprise and the impersonal characteristics of mechanical and automated operations.

According to a report by a Nikkeiren study group of business experts on "Ability-Oriented Management—Its Theory and Practice, 1969,"[4] ability-oriented labor management consists of the harmonization of economic nationality with a respect for humanity. With regard to the latter, the report states that this includes the identification of employee abilities, the development of their abilities in full, the provision for opportunities, positions and environments for the use of these abilities and appropriate treatment of employees. In order to achieve these results, the report states that Japanese management has added labor management innovation to its emphasis on technological innovation. Although the aim might be an eventual changeover from seniority-based management to ability-oriented management applicable to all employees, initially the primary emphasis has been on changing the system for supervisors and middle managers.

In 1971, the collapse of the international monetary system based upon the U.S. dollar caused a slight depression in Japan and forced management to think in terms of change. One such change was a consideration of management by participation as a further extension of the concept of ability-oriented management. To the Japanese, management by participation meant a system which integrates the goals of an enterprise with those of each individual participating in the management. In the United States and Europe, management by participation has generally meant joint consultation between management and labor. In Japan, this type of consultation takes place in what is called a "works council." In some cases, Japanese industry has used the concept of a junior board of directors for special types of participation in management. Included within the Japanese concept of management by participation is management by objectives whereby each worker or group of workers set up objectives for himself as part of achieving the total goals of the enterprise. Quality control groups and the zero defects system are also being employed by some Japanese companies as a further extension of the philosophy of management by participation.

In order to be able to participate in management, employees need training in the kind of knowledge, skills and attitudes which are required for participative management. Much of the training undertaken by Japanese companies in the past has been conducted within the organization itself. A survey by the Japan Industrial Training Association in 1971 indicated that many companies are also encouraging self-development. This survey of 855 Japanese firms found that the following means were being employed for self-development:
1. inquiry and agency services for extramural courses and seminars, 62 percent
2. the distribution of teaching texts and other materials for self development, 45 percent
3. the preparation and distribution of lists of recommended publications, 33 percent
4. the provision for courses and seminars on an optional basis, 27 percent
5. economic support for voluntary groups for self development, 27 percent
6. economic support for voluntary individuals for self-development, 22 percent
7. service for voluntary training groups, 22 percent
8. contacts on the results of studies on self-development, 15 percent
9. self-evaluation and superior guidance through interviewing, 15 percent[5]

Other management concepts being introduced into Japan are organization development and job enlargement or job enrichment. Organization development concepts patterned after those of American Telephone and Telegraph have been adopted by a number of Japanese companies including public utilities, chemical producers, manufacturers of electrical appliances, sales companies, and financial organizations. Several companies have restructured operations to provide job enrichment and enlargement. Similarly, the shift from seniority-based labor management to ability-oriented management will tend to relate wages more to ability or function rather than seniority.

With regard to the role of women in management, Japanese business still considers women only for lower positions of a production, clerical, or retailing nature. The primary change with regard to women has resulted in the expansion of Japanese international operations. In the past, the wives of Japanese businessmen have not been included in social activities in connection with business appointments. As Japanese businessmen deal internationally they find that the inclusion of their wives in social functions is expected along with the wives of their foreign counterparts. However, the older Japanese wives still hesitate to mix with strangers or foreigners. The younger generation, on the other hand, enjoys mixing and realizes that their smiles and handshaking help their husbands in business. In addition, more and more Japanese are living or travelling overseas with their wives, thus making the latter more cosmopolitan. Since many of these families are of the younger generation, it is expected that wives of Japanese managers in the future will know at least one foreign language and will have had the experience of living or travelling abroad.

International expansion of Japanese business, changes in value systems and customs, and the continued adaptation of new managerial techniques to meet the needs of a growing society has placed a strain on traditional Japanese management philosophies and practices. The type of management which is capable of adapting rapidly to the changing sociocultural value systems of Japan has been referred to as "ultra-rationalism" management.[6] According to Masatoshi Yoshimura, General Counselor of Sanyo Chemical Industries, Ltd., the elements of this type of management are:

1. Strong Creativity
    A special mental ability which always causes to invent unique modes of management, exploitation of new business fields untapped by others, creation of high yield merchandises useful to the society, and so on. The creativity is half nature-gifted, but can be developed posteriorly by training through the hard and trying management careers.
2. Intuitive Ability
    This is an ability to see through many complicated management problems and sense the required conclusions instantaneously which eventually turn out to be true and correct.

3. Prophesying Ability
    Ability to prophesy the social and business trend of 5-10-20 years ahead as if he sees it on the palm.
4. Pioneering Spirit
    Ability to readily explore into unknown fields with courage and conviction, based on the conclusions derived from the above 1, 2, and 3.
5. Accommodative Ability
    Ability to evaluate and bring up the subordinates always on fair and square basis without regards to special personal relations and favoritism and accommodate everyone indiscriminately.
6. Selfless Love
    He must continuously develop an urge for love which is entirely free from egocentricity which is the most formidable enemy of the top management.
7. Personal Magnetism
    When all of the above conditions are fulfilled, there will be generated 'personnel magnetism' which enchants and attracts all persons in the corporation and also attracts third persons. In some cases it also tends to attract other companies which having business or technical relations in one way or others, are willing to work with or under this company.
    In this case, it can be called 'company magnetism.'
8. Service to the Society
    The natural duty of an enterprise for the foundation of its existence.[7]

Many of these suggested characteristics are the same as those which have been part of Japanese management throughout the country's development and which have proved effective.

LABOR

In addition to those characteristics which may be appropriate for the overall guidance of the firm, Japanese management is also faced with a labor shortage in the 1970s. This shortage is resulting in a rather high turnover rate particularly among the younger workers and among the highly skilled. Although the small and medium-sized enterprises which tend to pay low wages have had the most difficult time in recruiting and retaining workers, even the large companies with high wage and lifetime employment policies have had problems of this kind. Since 1970, the labor supply in Japan has been decreasing and wages have risen to a level whereby the cost per unit of work is comparable to that of the European countries. A survey by Japan's Ministry of Labor has indicated that the annual increase in the labor population which averaged 870,000 between 1965 and 68 will decrease to 580,000 between 1968 and 75.[8] Such a change will result in an increase in the relative number of older workers, thereby resulting in a further increase in wage costs if the traditional seniority system is used as the basis for wage increases and promotions. The introduction of the five-day work week in Japan has also resulted in a further increase in the labor cost per unit of output.

One of the means being considered by both large and small Japanese enterprises to cope with the labor shortage is the expansion of production overseas particularly in the countries of Southeast Asia where there is an abundant labor force. Because of environmental problems, crowded conditions and the high cost of living in Japan itself, it is not anticipated that Japanese industry will import labor from other Southeast Asian countries. It is much less costly in the long run to relocate the industry in the developing nation where costs not only of labor but also of other factors is much less than that in Japan.

With regard to the cost of labor, the Japan Federation of Employers Association conducted a survey to 2,282 managers of enterprises in the Tokyo area asking them how they planned to cope with increased wage costs.[9] Of those surveyed, 65 percent indicated that drastic action was needed to compensate for increased labor costs. Concerning such action, 32.7 percent advocated the rationalization of unprofitable divisions of the company, 32.5 percent suggested shifting to more profitable merchandise, 23.3 percent recommended large-scale investments in labor saving machinery, 22.4 percent were in favor of rationalizing the total operation and 20.7 percent felt that the solution was to raise prices. Most of those advocating a raise in price as a solution were from the small and medium-sized enterprises where managers appeared to be less innovative and rationalization-oriented than those of the large companies.

FORECASTING THE FUTURE

Many of Japan's problems with regard to its labor force, pollution control, changing export potentials, and raw materials have been attributable to management decision-making which concentrated on the present conditions and their exploitation for growth and development. In the past, not enough attention was devoted to forecasting and the use of computer-based mass information systems. In order to make decisions in a rapidly changing social and economic environment, Japanese managers can no longer rely upon their intuitive judgment. To continue to progress they must develop scientific methods of forecasting and of storing information about past trends and present conditions.

With regard to forecasting, the Japan Society of Futurology was founded in 1968 with a foundation prospectus which stated as follows:

> Since the Meiji Restoration of a century ago, Japan has modernized herself at a pace nearly twice as fast as the Western nations. She therefore has had to undergo a correspondingly rapid-paced social change, which has made it particularly important for her to readjust her traditional social and cultural values and institutions to new needs of the times. In the years ahead, too, Japan with her teeming population within the confines of a limited land area will continue to be faced with a greater need than the rest of the world to accurately foresee what the future has in store for us, and the time has now come to lay a scientific groundwork for this mountainous task.[10]

Although Japanese managers have exerted efforts to forecast changes in technology and market conditions, many of the factors relating to intensified international competition, to pollution control, and other uncertainties were frequently not considered in making decisions affecting the future. For example, the Japanese petro-chemical industry became overexpanded in 1971 because it failed to anticipate changes taking place in technology and the market by adhering to the traditional concept of facilities investment. With an increasing awareness of industrial pollution, a new scientific approach to forecasting is needed to attempt to measure the impact of new and existing technologies particularly as they affect society as a whole. However, from the standpoint of top management, it is difficult to find solutions which protect the environment and, at the same time, achieve goals of maintaining profits, exploiting new markets, reducing production costs and developing new and competing products.

Although many companies have been inadequately equipped to forecast the problems of rapidly expanding industry and technological advancement, management systemization in Japanese business has progressed at an accelerated pace leading to the practical application of operations research techniques and a wide use of computers to plan management strategy. A systems approach to management with emphasis on forecasting is beginning to be used in Japan leading to the design and utilization of management information systems as a support for decision-making including, in some instances, simulation techniques in designing corporate models.

With regard to research and forecasting, Masaki Nakajima, President of Mitsubishi Steel Manufacturing Company and the Mitsubishi Research Institute has suggested the following:

> Japanese society in the 1970s will enter the stage of "social-econ-industrial society" or "mass-informaindustrial society" or "mass-information producing, processing and consumption society" in which we observe the values of an industrial society concerning production of materials will be secondary to values concerning information and knowledge. This implies that Japanese society in the future will place a special stress upon certain types of industries whose production is information or knowledge; i.e., a shift of direction of the Japanese economy from a tertiary economy to a "quaternary" economy whose character is to provide service industries with knowledge and information. At the same time manufacturing industries will move from mere production industries to information intensive industries which produce technologically sophisticated goods. These trends will introduce radical change to the structure of Japanese industry and will necessitate its reorganization.
>
> What we will see in the mass-information society are various structural changes: social needs will shift from materials to services, and then further, from services to information and knowledge; and industries will progress from material-production to material-processing, and then also, from processing to systematization.[11]

The increased use of computers by both business and government in Japan has stimulated the pooling of information concerning technological innovations, forecasts, research, housing, and pollution control. Information corporations are expanding in Japan for the development of software and research institutes are not only active in software but also in research in the broader fields of economics, industry, technology, and society. It is anticipated that the Japanese government will also undertake various research projects on a large scale and integrate them with those of private enterprise.

The general trading companies have also undertaken radical reforms in their personnel, management organization and information systems. Their activities in the international markets have stimulated their development of up to date information systems designed for the processing of plans and information to be used by their top management.

INTERNATIONAL ASPECTS

Japan's shift from a debtor to a creditor nation has resulted in a number of changes with regard to governmental policies affecting international trade and investment, and the policies and practices of Japanese enterprise. The liberalization of foreign investment and the securities markets have brought about changes in international investment and capital movements and Japan's role as an international economic force in the world community. The Japanese general trading firms in going abroad in search of natural resources, labor, new markets and plant sites have created Japan-based multinational business organizations. Japan's business investment overseas has caused increased emphasis to be placed on international personnel administration, assistance to developing nations, possible mergers with other multinationals, and new thinking about the role of Japanese business in international cooperation.

The liberalization of foreign investment in Japan has opened the door for multinational companies to enter Japan in most all categories of business except for public utilities and strategic technologies such as aircraft, weapons, explosives, and space development. Since Japan has been finding it difficult to import advanced technology without foreign capital participation, it is anticipated that the decontrol of foreign investment should result in even more advanced technology reaching Japan. The competition of foreign firms in Japan's domestic market should stimulate further improvement in Japanese management and marketing techniques. On the other hand, Japanese business does fear that decontrol may bring some of the domestic enterprises under foreign domination and might eventually lead also to a monopoly of foreign interests in certain important fields where they control the patents on the technology. In general, Japanese industry feels that it still has a problem of catching up with the United States and Europe in research for the development of new technologies, in distribution of goods and services and in the efficiency of its management. Perhaps Japanese businessmen feel this because they are far behind their western counterparts in overseas production and sales. However, Japan's overseas business is growing rapidly and is providing strong competition in the international economic community.

In addition to the expanding role of Japanese business overseas, the shift in Japan's economic structure from that of a capital-importing debtor country to that of a capital-exporting creditor country has led to the internationalization of the Japanese securities business.[12] In 1971, Japan lifted restrictions on investments in foreign securities by Japanese investment trusts, institutional establishments such as life and property insurance companies, corporations, and private citizens making it possible for Japanese investors to acquire stocks listed on foreign exchanges. In September, 1971, transactions were further liberalized by the issuance of Japanese securities in foreign currencies and the expansion of Japanese securities companies' operations into foreign markets. At the same time, foreign securities companies were permitted to enter Japan and Merril-Lynch of the United States was the first to open an office in Tokyo. Also in 1971, Japan's Securities Transaction Law was amended to permit the taking over of corporate control through off-the-market purchase of stock shares in an open bid. Within certain restrictions, the sale of foreign securities investment trusts was also permitted. Further internationalization of Japan's securities markets resulted from the issuance of yen-based Asian Development Bank bonds, foreign government bonds such as those of Australia, and Eurodollar bonds. As a result of this liberalization and internationalization of the Japanese securities market, the total amount of capital raised in Japan in 1972 was $237 million. As Japan develops a better distribution system for securities, it is expected that the number of both foreign and domestic stocks listed on the Tokyo Stock Exchange will increase.

With regard to the foreign operations of Japanese securities firms, they had 50 overseas offices in 1973. In commenting on the future of the Japanese securities operations abroad, Segawa, Chairman of the Nomura Securities Company stated as follows:

> .... the U.S. maintains a monetary system under which long- and short-term financial services are separated and, therefore, Japanese securities companies' operations in that country are confined to transactions in securities. In Europe, on the other hand, securities business and banking services are generally combined into merchant banking institutions whose operations range from transactions in securities to the advance of long-term loans. It is therefore expected that Japanese securities companies will take a two-pronged strategy in expanding their operations network in the European countries, that is, establishment of local subsidiaries and joint venture with leading local banks.
>
> In the developing countries of Southeast Asia and elsewhere, meanwhile, it will be necessary at the current stage to concentrate efforts on developing long-term capital markets there except in a few instances. As most of these countries, though endowed with rich natural resources, are mostly suffering from a shortage of development funds, it is essential for Japanese securities companies entering these countries to endeavor, above everything else, to respect the nationalistic sentiments of the

local interests. In this sense, in order to gain smooth entree into the local monetary circles, it seems advisable for the Japanese firms to form joint ventures with established local banks whenever practicable, bearing in mind our obligation as one of the advanced nations to assist the developing nations in their efforts to lay the groundwork for the sound growth of their own capital markets.[13]

The Tokyo market will become increasingly important as a source of raising capital for Pacific regions. It is anticipated that not only Japanese companies will use the Market but also American and European enterprises seeking capital for ventures in the Far East and elsewhere.

With regard to international expansion of Japanese enterprises, it is anticipated that Japanese private overseas investment will reach $10 billion by 1975 and as much as $25 billion by 1980. Factors stimulating this rapid increase have been Japan's balance of payments surplus; the rise in its international competitive and capital strength, the increase in labor costs in Japan, and trend of restrictions on Japanese imports by other countries, and the development of sources for raw materials. In the future, Minoru Masuda, Director of the Trade and Development Bureau of the Ministry of International Trade and Industry believes that "half of the Japanese private overseas investment will be directed mostly by enterprises in the manufacturing category to develop and obtain natural resources in the developing countries, and a part of the remaining half will go in manufacturing enterprises of other advanced countries."[14]

In the expansion of Japan's international investment and trade, the general trading firms with their network of overseas offices have played a key role. Although there are about 6,500 trading companies in Japan, only ten can be classified as general trading firms which purchase and sell all kinds of commercial goods worldwide. These ten firms handle about 50 percent of Japan's total exports and 60 percent of her imports. The total volume of these ten firms approximated $86 billion in 1972, of which about half consisted of international transactions including exports from and into Japan and between third countries.[15] These ten firms had about 5,000 Japanese stationed in their more than 800 overseas offices which employed about 18,000 foreign nationals. The number of foreign enterprises in which these firms had made direct investments ranged from 10 to 140 each. By the end of 1972, one of the leading Japanese general trading companies had direct investments in 130 projects in 30 countries totalling $350 million. The multinational firms of Japan are the general trading companies such as Mitsui, Mitsubishi, and Nissho Iwai. It is these firms which maintain a wealth of information about business conditions, markets, and practices in the countries in which they have offices. The general trading companies play an active role in assisting Japanese companies in overseas business negotiations, in organizing joint ventures, in arranging the necessary financing and services in the supply of plant equipment, raw materials, and in the marketing of the finished product. Japan's general trading firms, therefore, are major participants in many of the Japanese overseas joint ventures.

Many of these Japanese investments and joint ventures overseas have resulted in international specialization which has advanced beyond trade transactions to include complex manufacturing, technology, research, and development. The economic and industrial structure of Japan itself, as previously indicated, is made up of heavy industry and large companies surrounded by small and medium-sized entities, thereby making it a combination of the types existing in both the advanced and the developing countries. The large enterprises of the United States and Europe have been interested utilizing Japan as a manufacturing or parts production base as a vertical form of international specialization and in forming joint ventures with Japanese business for manufacturing equipment as a horizontal form of international specialization. With regard to developing nations, many Japanese concerns have formed joint ventures with local companies particularly in Southeast Asia to serve as subcontractors, producers, and distributors for the Japanese parent.

Examples of large multinational enterprises using the Japanese joint venture to supply world markets include Komatsu International, a joint venture between Komatsu and International Harvester of the United States; Caterpillar Mitsubishi, a joint venture between Mitsubishi Heavy Industries and Caterpillar Tractor of the United States; and Taito Pfizer, jointly owned by Taito, Charles Pfizer of the United States and the Roche group in Switzerland. Japanese firms have also joined with foreign firms in advanced countries to manufacture Japanese products. For example, in the case of electronic desk calculators, Sharp has tied up with Swiss, Swedish, and United States manufacturers; Ricoh with a company in West Germany; Canon with a United States manufacturer; and Matsushita Communications Industrial with a West German firm.[16]

As previously indicated, the internationalization of Japanese manufacturing is usually promoted by the major general trading companies. In this connection, Nissho-Iwai and Mitsubishi Shoji have undertaken new types of international specialization; the former with the Tata Financial Group of India to sell chemical equipment in the Middle East and Southeast Asia, and the latter with French and Italian chemical engineering and construction companies to export large industrial plants to Africa, East Europe, the Middle East, and other regions. With regard to the developing nations, Japanese companies are increasingly utilizing firms in Korea, Hong Kong, Taiwan, and other Southeast Asian countries as processing plants, subcontractors, and export bases for such items as automotive parts, automobiles, textiles, foodstuffs, machinery parts, and printing, most of which are growth industries requiring a high concentration of manpower. These trends indicate a rapid growth of the internationalization of Japanese industry in the future.

With regard to Japanese overseas ventures, the expansion which has taken place in the developing countries has required economic and technical assistance in the daily operations of the overseas company. Initially, Japan's overseas financial aid program began mainly through its private industry and the offering of export credits as a means of promoting external trade. The main part of the Japanese government assistance prior to 1970 was in fulfillment of her reparations obligations stemming from World War II. Japan's aid in the 1970s has not been tied to her export promotion efforts as much as in the past, but has been an endeavor to draw up a cooperative program which will efficiently fill the needs of developing nations. Similar to other aid giving nations, Japan is disturbed by the fact that economic aid is not always used efficiently and for the best projects, but she also recognizes that it would be politically inexpedient to seek participation in the economic planning of the developing nations. Japan is hoping that the World Bank or other authoritative and impartial international organizations will play a more active role in advising and evaluating the economic plans of the developing nations so it will be easier for Japan to appraise the amount of aid truly needed to make these plans effective. Japan's plans are to cooperate primarily with these international organizations such as the World Bank not only in supplying funds but also the needed personnel.[17]

With regard to assistance to developing nations, which was a main topic of discussion at the UNCTAD meeting in Chile in 1972, Japan agreed, at that meeting, to make an effort to increase her development assistance to a maximum of 0.7 of her GNP. Japan's economic aid to developing nations was $2.14 billion in 1971 which was second only to that of the United States. However, only about $500 million of Japan's assistance was strictly governmental aid; the balance was mostly in the form of export credits for deferred payments.[18] Japan agreed to take steps to improve her foreign aid program, to abolish the strings attached, to increase the number of countries and types of goods qualified for aid, and, in general, to relax the conditions of her official development assistance.

With regard to the supplying of personnel for development assistance, the Japanese government has supported the program of the International Management Cooperation Committee of the International Management Association of Japan. The functions of this committee are to place Japanese volunteer executives in developing countries. By 1972, six years after its founding, the Committee had sent 159 executives to sixteen countries of Southeast Asia, Central and South America. In 1971, the Committee held a symposium in Tokyo with representatives from eleven Asian countries to discuss the performance and results of the first five years of this cooperative effort and to seek suggestions for improvement.[19] The favorable comments of the representatives of the developing nations at this meeting would indicate that the program of the IMCC makes a valuable contribution and that it will continue as part of the development assistance programs of Japan.

Most of the training of the local nationals who work for Japanese affiliated firms in the developing countries is undertaken by the Japanese parent company rather than through any official government assistance program. These Japanese companies have found it relatively easy to train technical personnel but have had difficulty in developing local managers who can adapt to and understand the Japanese management philosophy and methods. As a result, Japanese firms overseas have staffed their managerial positions with Japanese. One of the chief criticisms made against Japanese companies by Thailand, Indonesia, Korea, and the Philippines, has been about the practice of filling nearly all management positions in the local subsidiary with Japanese from the home office with the result that the local nationals have to be content with menial tasks. American companies, on the other hand, have adopted the opposite policy of training local personnel and filling managerial positions with local nationals. In Japan, for example, at least half the American firms are staffed exclusively by Japanese. In all the big United States banks operating in Tokyo, there are only two Americans; whereas, a survey of Japanese banks in the United States indicated no Americans were in positions at the managerial level: all were staffed exclusively by Japanese.[20]

A continuation of a policy of staffing managerial positions abroad with Japanese will tend to hinder the long-run internationalization of Japanese enterprise. As long as Japan's overseas ventures were primarily for the securing of raw materials, Japanese managers alone could work effectively and profitably. However, with expansion into banking, production, and marketing in overseas countries, the Japanese overseas affiliate will need to bring local nationals into positions of responsibility if it wishes to keep abreast of local conditions and to achieve the confidence and support of the people of the country in which it is operating.

Although Japanese companies have found it difficult to fit foreign nationals into its decision-making process and its other business practices, the more progressive firms have recognized the need to make adaptations in their home office managerial behavior and practices when operating in a foreign culture. In the case of one Japanese company establishing a factory in a Southeast Asian country, the company brought with it the general management concept of thinking of its employees as if they were members of a family. Education and training of employees and the control of personnel were considered as important aspects of the nativization of the subsidiary's personnel. This proved helpful in creating the kind of attitudes necessary to support a modern industrial system. It also elevated technological skills, cultivated leadership and planning ability, and provided a booster for the self sustained industrialization of the country. Yet, in spite of all these efforts and training, the Japanese managers felt that the eventual shifting of management to exclusively local managers was a problem which was difficult to solve.

Japan's problems of internationalization are far from solved and are beginning to raise new problems in addition to the still unsolved domestic problems. International management has become a reality to Japan with its government assistance to developing nations, with its dependence upon overseas sources for raw materials and energy, and with its management of factories in foreign countries either alone or in cooperation with local entities. Internationalization has produced a need on the part of the Japanese to seek solutions to the social and technical problems common to the whole world.

In summary, Japan started its development one hundred years ago as a uniform race of people living in an island country in the Far East. Its absorption of western management and technology caused its transformation from a feudalistic agricultural economy to a highly industrialized, international country. Through innovative and imaginative leadership and an energetic, intelligent population it advanced to a position of approaching for its people the highest standard of living for any country in the world. Its future is assured if its managers can acquire global understanding, sensitivity, analytical ability, judgment, and insight in the international sphere comparable to that which they employed in the domestic development of the country. The ability to gather accurate information and use it effectively in guiding the future plans of the country and its enterprises will be essential to Japan's continued development. Japanese managers, in continuing to assume positions of responsibility will need to understand their function in relationship to society and the world. Some Japanese feel that strong powers of leadership in persuasion, execution, and drive combined with a certain amount of aggressiveness will be needed to synthesize the interrelated elements required for continued development. As a warning, too much aggressiveness in global economic expansion may lead to retaliatory measures which even the adaptive Japanese leader-managers may find beyond their ability to handle.

NOTES

1. Nobuo Noda, "The Social Responsibility of Japanese Corporations," Management Japan, vol. 6, no. 2 (1972): 6.
2. Norishige Hasegawa, "Environmental Problems and the Management," Management Japan, vol. 6, no. 2 (1972): 15.
3. See the New York Times, August 23, 1972, p. 10.
4. See Saburo Nakayama "Management by Participation in Japan," Management Japan, vol. 6, no. 4 and vol. 7, no. 1 (1973): 30-37.
5. Ibid., p. 35.
6. Masatoshi Yoshimura, "Rationalism Management and Ultra-rationalism Management," Management Japan, vol. 5, no. 4 (1972): 14-15.
7. Ibid.
8. Kaichiro Nishino, "Shifts in Japan's Business Mind," Management Japan, vol. 6, no. 1 (1972): 12.
9. See "Business Trends—Impact of the Labor Shortage in Japan," Management Japan, vol. 4, no. 2 (1970): 40.
10. Norishige Hasegawa, "The Importance of Integrating Forecasting and Futurology in Management Training Programs" (Paper presented to the CIOS XVI International Management Congress, Munich, October, 1972).
11. Masaki Nakajima, "Role of the Research Organization—Present and Future," Management Japan, vol. 5, no. 1 (1971): 12.
12. See Minoru Segawa, "Internationalization of Japan's Securities Market and its Future Outlook," Management Japan, vol. 6, no. 4 and vol. 7, No. 1 (1973): 6-8; and Takahiro Yamauchi, "Future Prospect of International Capital Movements and the Role of Japan," Management Japan, vol. 4, no. 4 (1971): 6-8.
13. Minoru Segawa, op. cit., p. 8.
14. Minoru Masuda, "The Present Situation and the Future Course of Japan's Overseas Investment," Management Japan, vol. 6, no. 2 (1972): 25.
15. See Bunichiro Tanabe, "Role and Functions of Japanese General Trading Companies," Management Japan, vol. 6, no. 4 and vol. 7, no. 1 (1973): 14-16. and Yoshio Tsuji, "Japanese Trading Firms in the Age of Multinational Business," Management Japan, vol. 6, no 4 and vol. 7, no. 1 (1973): 18-19.
16. "Diversification of International Division of Labor in North and South," Management Japan, vol. 4, no. 2 (1970): 42.
17. See Kiyohisa Mikanagi, "Economic Cooperation in the Years Ahead," Management Japan, vol. 6, no. 2 (1972): 22-23.
18. Tsuneo Ichikawa, "Shifts in World Trading Partnership and Their Impacts," Management Japan, vol. 6, no. 3 (1973): 17.

19. See "An International Symposium on Management Cooperation," Management Japan, vol. 5, no. 3 (1971): 8-9; and "The Activities and Future Direction of IMCC As It Faces a Period of Transition," Management Japan, vol. 6, no. 1 (1972): 13-15.

20. Howard F. Van Zandt, "Japanese Management Practices in an International Perspective," Management Japan, vol. 6, no. 4 and vol. 7, no. 1 (1973): 28.

BIBLIOGRAPHY

BOOKS

Abegglen, James C., ed. Business Strategies for Japan. Tokyo: Sophia University, 1970.

Adams, T. E. M. and Kobayashi, N. The World of Japanese Business. Tokyo: Kodansha International Ltd., 1969.

Ali, Zaman, and Baset. Economic Development of Japan. Dacca: Ideal Library, 1967.

Allen, George C. Japan as a Market and Source of Supply. New York: Pergamon Press, 1967.

──────. A Short History of Modern Japan 1867-1937. New York: Praeger, 1963.

American Management Association. Doing Business in and with Japan. New York: 1969.

Ballon, Robert J. Doing Business in Japan. Tokyo: Sophia University, 1967.

──────, ed. The Japanese Employee. Tokyo: Sophia University, 1969.

──────. Joint Ventures and Japan. Tokyo: Sophia University, 1967.

Bieda, Ken. The Structure and Operation of the Japanese Economy. New York: Wiley, 1970.

Broadbridge, Seymour A. Industrial Dualism in Japan. Chicago: Aldine Publishing Co., 1966.

Brzezinski, Zbieniew K. The Fragile Blossom: Crisis and Change in Japan. New York: Harper & Row, 1972.

Chamberlain, Basil H. Japanese Things. Rutland, Vt.: Tuttle, 1971.

Corbet, Hugh, comp. Trade Strategy and the Asia Pacific Region. London: Allen and Unwin, 1970.

Craig, Albert M. and Shively, Donald H. Personality in Japanese History. Berkeley: University of California Press, 1970.

DeMente, Boye. How to Do Business In Japan: A Guide for International Businessmen. Los Angeles: Center for International Business, Pepperdine University, 1972.

Dening, Sir Maberly S. Japan. New York: Praeger, 1961.

DiMock, Marshall E. The Japanese Technocracy. New York: Walker/Weatherhill, 1968.

Downs, Ray F. Japan Yesterday and Today. New York: Praeger, 1970.

Glazer, Herbert. The International Businessman in Japan. Tokyo: Sophia University, 1968.

Goodman, Grant K. Davao, A Case Study in Japanese-Philippine Relations. Lawrence: University of Kansas, 1967.

Guillain, Robert. The Japanese Challenge. Philadelphia: Lippincott, 1970.

Hall, John W. and Beardsley, Richard K. Twelve Doors to Japan. New York: McGraw-Hill, 1965.

Hay, Kieth, A. Japan, Challenge and Opportunity for Canadian Industry. Montreal: Private Planning Association of Canada, 1971.

Hellman, Donald C. Japan and East Asia. New York: Praeger, 1972.

Hollerman, Leon. Japan's Dependence on the World Economy. Princeton: Princeton University Press, 1967.

Huh, Kyung-Mo. Japan's Trade in Asia. New York: Praeger, 1966.

Isenberg, Irwin, comp. Japan: Asian Power. New York: Wilson, 1971.

Ishida, Takeshi. Japanese Society. New York: Random House, 1971.

Japanese National Commission for UNESCO. Japan, Its Land, People, and Culture. 3rd ed. Tokyo: University of Tokyo Press, 1973.

Kahn, Herman. The Emerging Japanese Superstate: Challenge and Response. Englewood Cliffs: Prentice-Hall, 1970.

Kitamura, Hiroshi. Psychological Dimensions of U.S.-Japanese Relations. Cambridge: Center for International Affairs, Harvard University, 1971.

Kobayashi, Shigeru. Creative Management. New York: American Management Association, 1971.

Kojima, Kiyoshi. Japan and a Pacific Free Trade Area. London: MacMillan, 1971.

Kurihara, Kenneth K. The Growth Potential of the Japanese Economy Baltimore: John Hopkins Press, 1971.

Lal, Chaman. Japan Shows the Way. New Delhi: Indian Council of World Affairs, 1967.

Lockwood, William W. The State and Economic Enterprise in Japan. Princeton: Princeton University Press, 1965.

McNulty, Nancy G. Training Managers, the International Guide. New York: Harper and Row, 1969.

Maddison, Angus. Economic Growth in Japan and the U.S.S.R. New York: W. W. Norton, 1969.

Michio, Nagai. Higher Education in Japan. Tokyo: University of Tokyo Press, 1971.

Mikes, George. The Land of the Rising Yen: Japan. Boston: Gambit, 1970.

Moulton, Harold G. Japan: An Economic and Financial Appraisal. New York: AMS Press, 1969.

Nakane, Chie. Japanese Society. Berkeley: University of California Press, 1970.

Okita, Saburo. Post-War Japan's Rapid Economic Growth and Its Causes. Tokyo: Association of International Education, 1966.

Olson, Lawrence A. Japan in Postwar Asia. New York: Praeger, 1970.

Osgood, Packard, and Badgley. Japan and the United States in Asia. Baltimore: Johns Hopkins University Press, 1968.

Price, Willard. The Japanese Miracle and Peril. New York: John Day Co., 1971.

Roberts, Dorothy E. A Scholar's Guide to Japan. Boston: Christopher Publishing House, 1969.

Sebals, William J. and Spinks, C. Nelson. Japan, Prospects, Options, and Opportunities. Washington: American Enterprise Institute for Public Policy Research, 1967.

Shinohara, Miyohei. Structural Changes in Japan's Economic Development. Tokyo: Kinokuniya Bookstore, Inc., 1970.

Stone, Peter B. Japan Surges Ahead: The Story of an Economic Miracle. New York: Praeger, 1969.

Tsuru, Shigeto. Essays on Economic Development. Tokyo: Kinokuniya Bookstore, Inc., 1968.

Uri, Pierre. Trade and Investment Policies for the Seventies. New York: Praeger, 1971.

Yamamoto, George K. and Ishida, Tsuyoshi. Selected Readings in Modern Japanese Society. Berkeley: McCutchan Publishing Corp, 1971.

Yamamura, Kozo. Economic Policy in Postwar Japan. Berkeley: University of California Press, 1967.

Yoshino, M. Y. Japan's Managerial System: Tradition and Innovation. Cambridge: MIT Press, 1968.

MONOGRAPHS AND PERIODICALS

Noda, Nobuo. How Japan Absorbed American Management Methods. Asian Productivity Organization, Tokyo: 1969.

Socio-Economic Institute, Sophia University. More than 30 monographs on topics relating various aspects of Japanese business and joint ventures.

Management Japan published quarterly by the International Management Association of Japan in Tokyo. This periodical is in English and contains articles by leading Japanese business executives, government officials, and scholars on topics relating to Japanese Management.

ABOUT THE AUTHOR

ALLEN B. DICKERMAN is Director of the International Management Development Department at Syracuse University. He has taught at the Harvard Business School and the University of Rochester and has served as advisor on business affairs to various institutions in South America, Indonesia, and the Philippines.

His articles have appeared in such respected journals as <u>Personnel</u>, <u>Temas Administrativas</u>, and the <u>Harvard Business Review</u>.

Dr. Dickerman received his B.A. from Hamilton College, his M.B.A. from Harvard University, and his Ph.D. from Syracuse University.

RELATED TITLES
Published by
Praeger Special Studies

JAPANESE PRIVATE ECONOMIC DIPLOMACY:
An Analysis of Business-Government Linkages
William E. Bryant

JAPAN: FINANCIAL MARKETS AND THE
WORLD ECONOMY
Wilbur F. Monroe

THE CONTROL OF IMPORTS AND FOREIGN
CAPITAL IN JAPAN
Robert S. Ozaki

MARKETING IN JAPAN: A Management Guide
Michael Y. Yoshino